The Kama Sutra Diaries

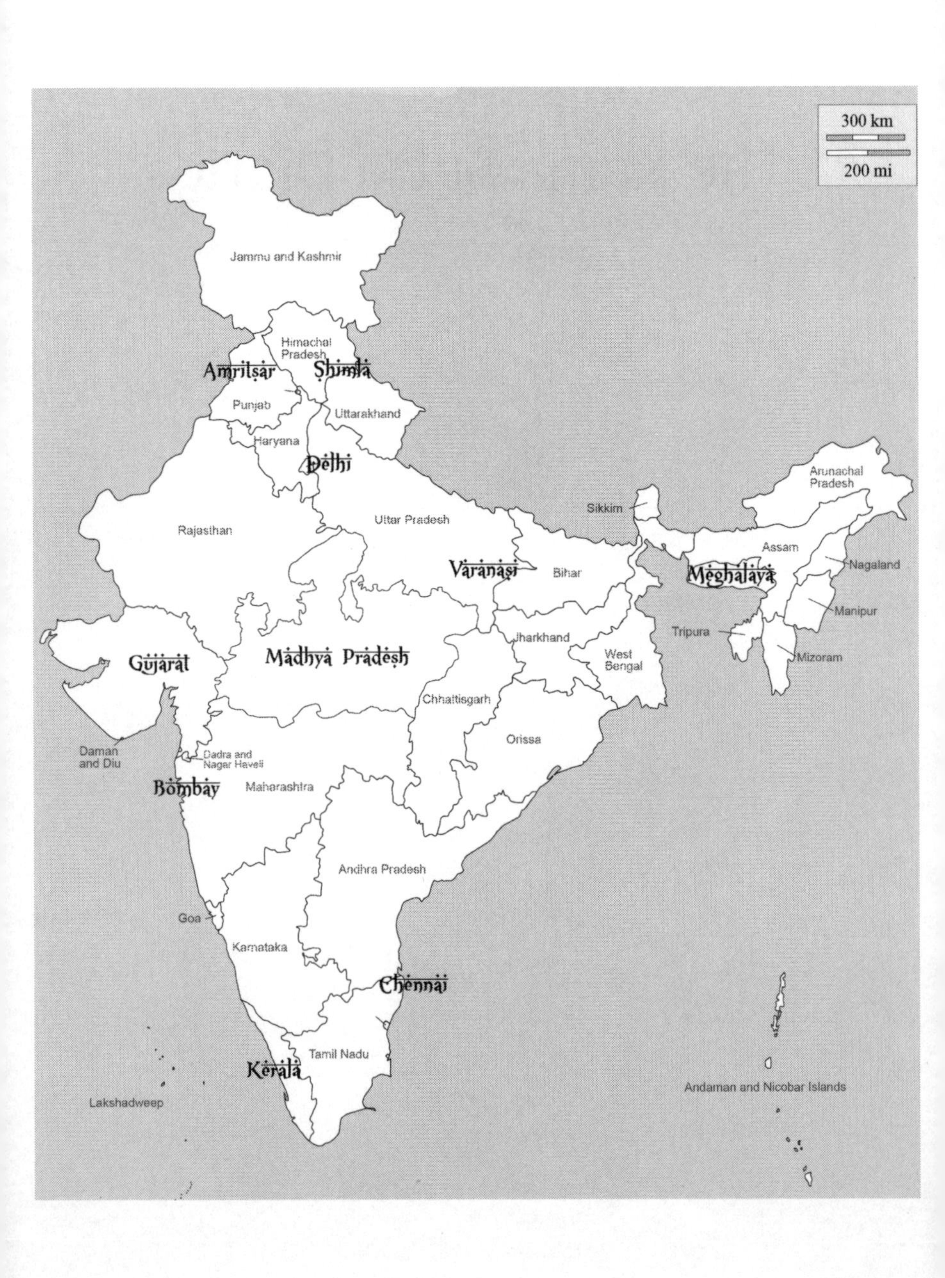
300 km
200 mi
Jammu and Kashmir
Himachal Pradesh
Amritsar
Shimla
Punjab
Uttarakhand
Haryana
Delhi
Arunachal Pradesh
Sikkim
Rajasthan
Uttar Pradesh
Assam
Varanasi
Bihar
Meghalaya
Nagaland
Manipur
Tripura
Jharkhand
West Bengal
Mizoram
Gujarat
Madhya Pradesh
Chhattisgarh
Orissa
Daman and Diu
Dadra and Nagar Haveli
Bombay
Maharashtra
Andhra Pradesh
Goa
Karnataka
Chennai
Tamil Nadu
Kerala
Lakshadweep
Andaman and Nicobar Islands

The Kama Sutra Diaries

Intimate Journeys through Modern India

Sally Howard

First published by
Nicholas Brealey Publishing in 2013

3–5 Spafield Street
Clerkenwell, London
EC1R 4QB, UK
Tel: +44 (0)20 7239 0360
Fax: +44 (0)20 7239 0370

20 Park Plaza
Boston
MA 02116, USA
Tel: (888) BREALEY
Fax: (617) 523 3708

www.nicholasbrealey.com

ISBN: 978-1-85788-589-7
eISBN: 978-1-85788-960-4

British Library Cataloguing in Publication Data
A catalogue record for this book is available from the
British Library.

Map of India on page ii based on the following courtesy of
d-maps.com:
http://d-maps.com/carte.php?num_car=24854&lang=en
http://d-maps.com/carte.php?&num_car=24859&lang=en

Printed in Finland by Bookwell.

Contents

Preface

I first visited India in my early 20s. Like many Westerners, I was immediately smitten by the subcontinent's living history, colour and chaos. Like many too, I found myself being drawn back to the country, time and again. During what has now been a 15-year relationship with India, she has given me many things: giddy panoramas; masterclasses in remaining cool in the face of byzantine bureaucracy; my most exquisite meals; and my most baroque illnesses. Most of all, she has given me her stories.

As a travel and human-interest journalist, these stories started to inform the direction of my work. I began to specialise in writing about India. I reported on the women marchers of Bhopal, who annually walk 700 kilometres on bare feet to protest about a chemical tragedy that's left that city's women infertile and, in the cruel marketplace of their country, unmarriageable. I wrote about the mutinous ascent of the love marriage in Indian society, and the nation's newly vocal LGBT (lesbian, gay, bisexual and transgender) community, who are looking to India's rich history of sexual 'otherness' to make sense of their future.

Nevertheless, despite these forays, something still played on my mind. Many aspects of India continued to be elusive to my mind and pen. I was exercised by the puzzle that India and Indians present: societally, spiritually and above all sexually. This, after all, is the land that gave us the Kama Sutra, that treatise on the pleasures and techniques of sex that remains unsurpassed in human history. But it's also a part of the world that is wedded, as no other, to the notion of the loveless, arranged marriage. It's a land that houses women cloistered in purdah, but also matriarchal tribes who view men as an expedient for insemination and agricultural labour. It's a land where families bow down to a graphic depiction of a conjoined phallus and vagina, the Shivaling, but where couples are routinely attacked by the police for the indiscretion of holding hands in public.

The plan for this book, an attempt to investigate these social and sexual anomalies – my 'sexploration', if you like – began to take shape four years ago. I noticed a mood shift in India: young Indians were clogging up cisterns at call centres with spent condoms; they were watching more porn than any country on earth; and they were increasingly protesting against sexual violence in a backlash that continues to play out today. With India rising at breakneck speed, and much of the nation's social change occurring along the fault line of sex, gender and sexuality, I decided that for the journey you'll read about in the following pages, it was now or never.

My trip – by train, plane and autorickshaw – takes me from north to east to south across the great Indian landmass. From the forested heartlands of Madhya Pradesh I head north to the cool Himalayan foothills at Shimla, continue to the populous northern plains at Amritsar and Delhi, then head east to the ancient, Ganges-hugging city of Varanasi, and further east to mountainous Shillong, where Indian topography and culture merge with that of neighbouring Bangladesh, China and Nepal. From the east, I make my way south to fecund and sun-warmed Kerala and on to Chennai, a city as overheated as the young clients storming its busy sex clinics. I finish my journey in sultry Bombay (Mumbai), the Arabian Sea–facing metropolis that bristles with twenty-first-century ambition, where unions are forged online and where, in a sexed-up city-as-shopfront, anything goes.

My sexploration also looks back through the prism of time: first, two millennia, to the spiritual and philosophical seedbeds of the sexuality proposed by Vatsyayana's famous treatise and seen today, in all its exuberance, at the so-called Kama Sutra temples of Madhya Pradesh. Then, at Shimla, I turn to more recent history; to the period of the Victorian British colonialists whom the Indians call 'Britishers', three generations who strove to shape and contain Indian sexuality, and whose legacy, like that of India's ancient Sanskrit and spiritual tradition, lives on in both India and the West. I next look to the present day, attempting to capture a snapshot of a nation that's undergoing a seismic social shift.

I come to all of this as a journalist, and as a woman fascinated by social change. Yet I also, inevitably, view India's metamorphosing sexuality and sexual politics through my own, more personal perspective as a child of the Western sexual revolution. Buoyed by the invention of the contraceptive pill and by Second Wave feminism, my parents' generation created a brave new world, sexually and socially. They believed – and told us, their children – that we could have it all: free love if we so desired; marriage unfettered by economic necessity if we didn't. I explore why many of my generation feel disillusioned with this promise.

I also investigate the long-running pas de deux between Eastern and Western sexualities: from the days the earliest East India Company officials were struck by the 'succulent houris of the East' to the ripples caused by the arrival of a translated Kama Sutra in an England gripped by moralising late-Victorian crackdowns, and to the hippy 'freaks' who arrived in India in the 1960s, hoping the open carnality of ancient Hinduism would inform their own experience. I investigate how the sexual images and self-images of East and West have fed into and influenced one another, since Elizabeth I's emissaries from a cold and insignificant island were first captivated by the splendours of Mughal India.

I travel with a pair of parallel eyes, as her work and parenting duties permit: Dimple, a 32-year-old Delhiite. I first met Dimple in 2005, when I stayed at the hotel she then represented as a PR executive. She was, as Indian women can be, deliciously irreverent beneath her veneer of social propriety. Eight years later she is a good friend, and one of a small but growing number of women who has had the hutzpah to escape her unhappy arranged marriage. As such, she is the living embodiment of her country's societal shifts. So this trip is also, in part, an attempt to witness a changing India through the eyes of a woman whose personal happiness is invested in what her nation will become.

For a sense of the pace of change on the subcontinent, my journey coincides with Bollywood starlet Sherlyn Chopra becoming the first Indian woman to be photographed unclothed for *Playboy* magazine; Indian MPs being caught viewing porn while parliament was in session; and communal riots breaking out in cities across the land after a Muslim actress accused an Indian men's magazine of photoshopping in her nipples. And the augurings, of course, of the Delhi uprisings, in which tens of thousands of Indians protested against the prevalence and brutality of rape incidents in their capital.

On our journey, Dimple and I enjoy a few epiphanies about our respective formative histories, and we raise a few smiles – and some eyebrows. Above all, we attempt to lift the bed sheets on the phenomenon that's throbbing below it all like the battery-operated sex toys young couples are buying illegally from backstreet Delhi stalls: the Indian sexual revolution.

PART ONE: THE NORTH I

So, tell me how they used to do it

1 | POSITION IMPOSSIBLE, Madhya Pradesh

The erotic 'Kama Sutra temples' of Khajuraho

Kama is the enjoyment of appropriate objects by the five senses of hearing, feeling, seeing, tasting and smelling, assisted by the mind together with the soul. The ingredient in this is a peculiar contact between the organ of sense and its object, and the consciousness of pleasure which arises from that contact is called Kama.
—Kama Sutra, Chapter Two, On the Acquisition of Dharma, Artha and Kama, Burton translation, 1883

'See, over here – Kali,' says Ajay, our guide. 'Kali: the wild goddess. Kali: the goddess of time and change.'

We meet Ajay inside the entrance to the Western Complex of temples at Khajuraho, a small town in the central Indian state of Madhya Pradesh. It's a land-locked terrain of parched plains, scrub-covered hills and forest, boasting the unhappy achievement of heading India's state Hunger Index, and most visitors come here for the two Ts: the tigers at Bandhavgarh and Kanha National Parks, and the temples at sites such as Bhojpur; at Chitrakoot, the putative home of India's epic heroes, Rama and Sita (the tried and separated lovers of Hindu epic the Ramayana and incarnations of the gods Vishnu and Lakshmi); and at Khajuraho, where a complex of medieval Hindi structures has become, over the past two decades, India's second-most-visited tourist attraction after the Taj Mahal.

Ajay walks us to Kandariyâ Mahâdeva, the largest and most ornate of the temples in the Complex. Dressed in yellow flared trousers, he seems to glide as if mounted on castors across grass bleached gold-green in the blazing sun of the Indian plains.

'The creation myth of Kali says that her yoni, or vagina, fell to the earth on the sacred hill near Guwahati in Assam,' he continues. 'So in carvings you'll see her squatting, with her yoni peeled open. Often she squats above a phallus, representing Shiva's lingam, the holiest phallus; or she holds phalluses in her many hands. Kali is foremost among the goddesses of Tantric Hinduism, and what she shows us is that, at least in these earlier depictions, sex was central to Indian religion. Many people see Kali as the goddess of death, anger and destruction, but that's just a caricature. Kali was also always about sexuality, or a Hindu idea of sexuality; that is to say Shakti, or the creative feminine force. In the days of the Chandelas, and for many centuries before, the way to enlightenment was clear: it was through the worship of women's vaginas. This was the female principle, Mother Earth.'

A dynasty that commanded north India through the tenth to thirteenth centuries and emerged from the regions that are now Pakistan and Afghanistan, the Chandelas made their capitals at Khajuraho and, later, Mahoba, in modern-day Uttar Pradesh. But it was at Khajuraho that the Chandelas most indulged their passion – one that became defining of their dynasty – for carving sculptural art. At Khajuraho, in forest clearings, they created upwards of 80 intricately carved yellow sandstone temples in the beehive-like Nagara style, in which the temple deity womb-chamber is topped by a superstructure resembling a rugged mountain peak.

What marks the Nagara temples at Khajuraho out from the similar examples peppering the Indian subcontinent is their sculptural subject matter. The lowest-perimeter Khajuraho temples are, in effect, vast erotic storyboards. These range from the finely wrought works at Kandariyâ Mahâdeva, Vishvanatha and Lakshmana in the Western Group, which were constructed at the eleventh-century height of the Empire, to the cruder, later sculptural renditions of the Eastern Complex and further afield Southern Temples, when the waning Chandela Empire was riffing on its former glories in erotic imagination, and art.

Khajuraho's hundreds of metres of lusty friezes are peopled by a host of characters: animal, godly, human and their hybrids. Celestial nymphs, or apsaras, sprawl out their naked bejewelled bodies, apply make-up, wash their hair and repeatedly knot and unknot their girdles across the temple surfaces like so many punctuation marks. Ranks of griffins also appear frequently, as do naked, anthropomorphised guardian deities (the god Brahma, for example, as a lustful, pot-bellied voyeur). The main draw, however, is what we are here for: Khajuraho's elaborately interlocked love-making couples, or maithunas.

'Hah!' That lusty Indian exclamation that's somewhere between surprise and assent comes from my good friend Dimple, who's standing beside me. When I first met her she was what has latterly become known, derisively among Indian feminists, as a GIG, or Good Indian Girl, her life having trod the route of many girls of her upper middle-class background and caste: ladies' college followed by an arranged marriage to an engineer from the rich Punjabi capital, Chandigarh. She dressed the part, too: hair long and shining with jasmine oil, muted gold jewellery and crisp, businesslike sarees.

Today Dimple still dresses, as she puts it, 'arty smarty'. She abjures the jeanswear uniform of young metropolitan Indians for Mysore silk scarves and classy shalwar kameez, the knee-skimming shirt-and-trouser combination that's shorthand, in polite Indian society, for female modesty. However, in every other respect Dimple has evolved into something more interesting, edgy even: a divorcée single mum who's as unapologetic about her marital status as she is about her array of 'naughty' habits – Indian heavy metal; adding shots of gin to her nimbu pani; and that common weakness in a country in which 9 per cent of the population has type 2 diabetes, sugar.

In many ways Dimple is a pioneer: forging a path across the no man's land between Indian societal expectations and individual self-will; making her own choices, flouting the immense pressure to be the Good Indian Girl. She's certainly a canny operator in one of the most confusing and contradictory societies in which any woman can participate.

'Somewhere along the line,' Ajay starts up again, 'Hinduism lost Shakti. We kept our goddesses, but Shakti was lost. This was down to the one big idea shared by India's two conquering powers: patriarchy.'

The Muslims arrived first, in the south of the subcontinent. In their earliest campaigns, during the Golden Age of Islamic scholarship and trade, they were accepting of India's multiple deities, gods and goddesses both. But in the Mughal era (1526–1857 CE), specifically under emperor Aurangzeb (1618–1707), they became brutal. They repeatedly destroyed the 'shrine eternal', the Hindu temple at Somnath in Gujarat; and they vandalised the old goddesses, ransacking the Tantric temples to the yoginis, cutting off their breasts and yonis.

However, this wasn't the whole story by any means. As late as the early 1600s Muhammad Quli Qutb Shah (1580–1612), fifth sultan of the Qutb Shahi dynasty of diamond-rich Golkonda (part of modern-day Hyderabad) and a poet, penned lines such as this, in 'Basant' (a celebration of spring):

Her nipples beneath her dripping bra, like the sable night appear,
How can the night withstand the sun? I'm utterly mystified.

'Later, of course, the Britishers arrived in India,' Ajay continues, 'with a new idea of a heaven and earth where white men ruled. These influences brought about the Shivaiite Hinduism we see today, in which the male god Shiva, considered by many Hindus the supreme deity, plays a bigger role.'

It was during the high summer of the British Raj, when Britain itself was subject to an unprecedented wave of sexual repression, that the fame of the erotic temples at Khajuraho took flight. For several centuries, these complexes sat forgotten, reabsorbed by the thick central Indian forestland, untouched by the marauding Muslim Caliphates. Then, in 1863, they were discovered for our modern age by Alexander Cunningham, a general who was undertaking a survey of Madhya Pradesh as part of the British Raj's Archaeological Survey of India.

Cunningham, who conducted his surveys from the comfort of a palanquin carried by coolies, described the temple friezes he discovered at Khajuraho, in his report back to headquarters at Calcutta, as 'rather warm'. Later responses to the temples at Khajuraho were less understated. By the 1870s, the site had been determined a threat to 'public morality', with both Indian subjects and British dissuaded from visiting the complexes for fear that their blatant carnality would corrupt the women – the British memsahibs – charged with maintaining civilised sexual standards in the colonies.

'The Britishers called them the "Kama Sutra Temples",' continues Ahay, 'whereas in fact, the Kama Sutra isn't all sex, sex, sex.' He removes a handkerchief from his pocket and dabs his perspiring brow. 'It's just one of a collection of erotic and advice texts – the Kamashastra – on good and gracious living. The specific advice as to the seeking of kama, or pleasure, was aimed at the leisured playboy, or man about town, of the booming Gupta Empire. The text was composed at some point between the first and fifth centuries and is ascribed to a sage named Vatsyayana. We don't know much about him, except perhaps that he was celibate!'

'And who was the Victorian Britisher translator?' asks Dimple. 'He was taking a risk, wasn't he?'

'Sir Richard Burton,' continues Ajay, 'British Raj officer, scholar and adventurer. And it was a very risky business indeed. He and his fellow translator, a gentleman by the name of Arbuthnot, were almost imprisoned for their translation, so obscene was the text considered. Incredibly, Burton's translation, while widely circulated from the late nineteenth century, wasn't formally published in Britain and America until 1962!'

It was these postcards from India's sexually liberal past – the erotic art and literature caught under the umbrella category of the Kama Sutra – that would do so much to sharpen the Victorian stereotyping of the Indian subcontinent as morally lax. Soon it would lead to a crackdown on practices and ancient communities seen as representative of such looseness, such as the ancient tradition of tawaifs, or courtly concubines; the devadasi caste married to temple deities (and sometimes, though not always, engaged in prostitution); and the hijras, or eunuch caste.

In all-India censuses in 1868 and again in 1871, select groups that the Raj reformers wanted to monitor were focused on, including prostitutes, lepers and eunuchs (women, incidentally, were listed only by number per household, not by name). These castes began their slow and inevitable decline from respectability, although their communities endured. It was a downhill path for these increasingly embattled groups that could only lead in one direction: sex work.

In the frieze in front of us, the goddess Kali is less in a sexual position than part of a sexual tableau. Her breasts have been eroded, not by the invading forces of Islam, but by ten centuries of wear and tear. Yet elsewhere on her body, her lineaments are so well preserved she could have been carved last week.

On her head is a pointed hairdo that echoes the honeycomb temple spires of the temples that ring every blue horizon. At her shoulders are two naked apsara, heavenly nymphs, who sit cross-legged and play with their breasts, which are high and round like cantaloupe melons. At her feet, two griffins tug at their penises: the figure on the left simultaneously pleasuring a neighbour; the figure on the right, with his free hand, devouring a leaf.

'You'll know betel leaf,' says Ajay, extracting from his pocket a paan preparation, the Indian digestif in which betel leaf is wrapped around sweets and aromatics, such as coconut and rose-petal preserve. 'In India today we eat it like this, or real betel addicts will chew at the leaves on their own. But it's also always been an aphrodisiac. In the Kama Sutra a couple is advised to prepare for sex by rubbing each other's bodies in sandalwood ointment and feeding betel to one another; like, I suppose, how you in the West use body oil and champagne.'

We continue around the back of Kandariyâ Mahâdeva, to a parade of even more lusciously pornographic maithunas, on

Lakshmana temple. At the first, a woman's hand rests on a man's genitalia as, to their right, two men turn towards each other, tongues groping. At the next, a standing man copulates with a cross-legged woman, who's supported by two masturbating attendants. In another, a male fellates another male, who lies supine, as a griffin pulls a mischievous face.

As we stand, taking in this convoluted sexual scene, an Indian family of six walks past. It comprises two teenage sons, one in a high-necked Muslim-style shirt and the other a black Iron Maiden T-shirt, a daughter in thick spectacles, two conservative-looking parents and a grandmother who's wearing two layered cardigans and flip-flops teamed with socks.

As is usual in this nation where few feel there's an inherent rudeness in staring, the family stops and stares – not at the erotic friezes, but at the firangi looking at them. One of the sons pulls out a camera and demands of me 'one photo'. As it's taken he stands next to me stiffly, one hand perched on my shoulder, pointing at the uncompromising tableaux behind us with his outside arm.

Dimple tuts as the family retreats. The 'one photo' phenomenon – the regular interruption of our trips by Indian tourists beseeching us for a holiday snap with the tall white woman – never fails to irritate her. I wonder why. Is it that she sees such behaviour as rustic, a bad advertisement for her uncosmopolitan countrymen? I don't have time to ask. As they move away, she says, in an exaggerated whisper, 'This one reminds me of how I used to climb trees as a kid.'

She's pointing at a frieze of a couple whose limbs are bound round one another, like a Boy Scout's knot. The woman rests one of her feet on the foot of the man, the other against his thigh. One of her arms is braced behind his back for support as the other clings to his shoulder and neck; and, in a twist that's trademark Khajuraho, the couple is bracketed by a pair of acolyte deities, their faces contorted as if in agony or ecstasy and their penises in their hands. I reach into my rucksack for a book, shaking from its well-thumbed pages grains of pale sand, a souvenir from my last trip to Goa.

'It's one of the four main sexual embraces of the Kama Sutra,' I say. 'Listen: "She steps on his foot with her foot, places her other foot on his thigh or wraps her leg around him, with one arm gripping his back and the other bending down on his shoulder, and panting gently, moaning a little, she tries to climb him to kiss him..." It's called "Climbing the Tree".'

Dimple laughs in delight.

As we walk along the shaded far wall of Lakshmana, I remind myself of the Kama Sutra's other big three positions. There's the 'Twining Vine', which looks like what we'd call today a standing-up cowgirl. Then there's the 'Rice and Sesame', in which the couple's thighs and arms are entangled 'so tightly they seem to be wrestling with each other'; and the 'Milk and Water', a more recognisable position to Western eyes, in which the woman is seated on the man's lap, facing him.

At Khajuraho, as in the Kama Sutra, there's much that seems familiar in the depiction of sex, but also much that feels very different. For a start, there's a lot more on offer, in terms of sexual positions, than the stock moves of Western pornography, giving a sense that the pleasures of sex have narrowed rather than broadened in the hundreds of intervening years.

Ajay leads us to the jutting west corner of the temple and then, with a lightning grin, exclaims, 'Look, here's something showing what ancient Hindus can teach us about not taking sex and religion too seriously. It's Ganesh, the elephant god, wearing a broad smile. And what's he looking at?'

A voyeuristic Ganesh (Kirat Sodhi).

It's a trick of perspective. We round 90 degrees of the temple wall and see, behind Ganesh, a bald-headed Brahmin priest in flagrante with a court maiden, supplely doubled over, forehead to her knees. It becomes clear now that Ganesh is looking on: the self-congratulating voyeur. This playfulness would be unconscionable in the Judeo-Christian tradition or Islam, especially twenty-first-century Islam, undergoing the painful spasms of change.

So what was the original purpose of Khajuraho's unapologetic erotic art? No one really knows. Some say the maithunas were a sex education tool, something like a medieval *Joy of Sex*. Many academics point out that the maithunas decorate the lower panels of the temples but are absent from those higher up, and that they thus might depict low human impulses that need to be overcome in order to reach a higher spirituality and enlightenment. A third argument runs that they were designed to distract the gods from exhibiting their wrath during bad monsoons; still another that they're a pictorial storyboard representing the wedding night of the god Shiva and his second consort Parvati.

We sit on the high Jagati stone plinth of the Varaha temple. Behind us, framed by huge stone columns, is a temple deity in the shape of a giant stone boar: Varaha, or the third avatar of the Hindu god Vishnu, the supreme god in Vaishnavism, one of the four major branches of Hinduism. In front of us, from our elevated height, is a fine view of the Western Complex dotted with tourists and – on the horizon behind the temple silhouettes – of a purple-pink setting sun.

Our vantage point buys us a respite from the hawkers who've been tailing us for the past 15 minutes. Khajuraho's modern, ancillary tourist town does a brisk trade in sex for sale, from mildly inoffensive plastic memorabilia to the women and child prostitutes plying the transport hubs and, in a new trend, young male gigolos who solicit older female travellers in the town's tourist cafés.

'It's unlikely Khajuraho actually has anything to do with the Kama Sutra,' Ajay says now, crossing his flares for better purchase on the high plinth. 'In case you're wondering, the "kama" of the title doesn't refer to the concept of cause and effect, as many Westerners think, but to one of the four central Hindu purusarthas, or aims in life: sexual or erotic pleasure. The others are dharma, which is like duty, justice or social obligation; artha, which is about money, political power or success; and moksha, the goal sought at the end of a Hindu's life – spiritual liberation. Kama itself encompasses the sensual pleasures of food, perfume and music, so it's a much bigger concept than what is often believed today. Sutra literally means "thread", and refers to the punchy style of text, littered with aphorisms, which encourages rote learning or learning by heart.'

'Hah!' says Dimple again. 'We've lost so much understanding. Did you know that Sanskrit has over 20 words for sex? And that Hindi has words about sex that have no direct translation into English? There's chudasi, which means 'sadness after sex'; and meetha dard or 'sweet ache', which is like the heavy feelings in one's limbs after sex.

'We've lost so much,' she adds again dolefully, looking down at a group of teenagers in neat Christian school uniform, sniggering behind their hands at the friezes.

There's one more thing I want to ask Ajay about before we battle our way out of the temple complexes: Tantra. It's a word we've heard in passing several times today and is the aspect of Indian spiritual practice that's perhaps most misunderstood in the West. To Westerners, Tantra is best known for its sexual rites: the techniques of delaying orgasm made famous by Sting and Trudi Styler, for example.

When I mention this, Ajay sighs in exasperation. 'Tantrism is very misunderstood today, even in India,' he says. 'It was actually a method of religious practice whose rites dominated Hinduism, Jainism and Buddhism for over 700 years. You see, unlike previous traditions, which tended to describe the world as an illusion, Tantra celebrated and incorporated the earthly in its rites. So the here and now was to be embraced, rather than renounced. A very small number of these rites were based on the Shakti school of Tantra – Shakti, you see, again? This school believed that male energy could only become complete by being united with the female, spiritually and sexually.

'So, this is where the sexual rites come from,' he explained. 'As with many concepts in Indian religion, the good and bad come in the practice. So Shakti Tantrism gives us a celebration of human sexuality, but it also, as a downside, gave us the practice of forcing young women, *devadasis* devoted to god, to work as prostitutes at Tantric temples.'

Much as modern Indians protest – and they certainly do – about the Western sensationalism of Tantrism, there is ample corroborating material for a titillating approach. Consider the nitty-gritty, for example, of practices such as vajroli-mudra, in which the male initiate trains himself to draw the amrita, or intermingled male and female sexual fluids, back into his penis, like a phallic straw. Or the portfolio of practices aimed at arousing the Kundalini, the primal power of the central nervous system.

The anally focused techniques devised by Tantra to wake the 'coiled beast' of Kundalini include Tada Mudra (knocking one's buttocks on the ground); rolling a cotton ball under one's tailbone; and the key Tantric activation method of Adhorata, or anal sex. The principal aim in Adhorata is the ejaculation of semen into the rectum, which is said to nourish the Kundalini gland – believed to be housed between the rectal wall and the coccyx – 'like the white of an egg fertilises the yolk' and to sustain and arouse the resident Shakti. As late as the 1920s, exquisite 'anal technicians' proliferated in Indian prostitute castes, among the ei chou troupes of boy actors (who hailed from China) and the touring dancing boys of Ceylon (modern-day Sri Lanka, known throughout the nineteenth century for its male prostitution).

Dimple and I take Raja's leave at the Western Complex gates, bundling into the back seat of an autorickshaw that's chugging away expectantly, surrounded by touts. Inside its leaf-green and yellow trimmed exterior the vehicle boasts the usual accoutrements: a driver with a jumpy accelerator foot, a tinted-glass windscreen and thick rexine seat covers printed with cartoon images of strawberries. We pull away from the broken kerb and soon the sights and sounds of the city horns and hawkers fade to a whisper behind us, like crashing waves as you retreat from the shore.

As I stare out of the open doorway of the rickshaw at the dusty road blurring past, I think about how Khajuraho's frank carnality must have struck the Victorian British. Cunningham, after all, alighted at the temples at the height of the Purity Movement's grip on Britain. This was a late nineteeth-century social movement that sought to abolish prostitution and other sexual activities that were considered immoral. Composed primarily of women, the movement was active in English-speaking nations from the late 1860s to about 1910 and exerted an important influence on the contemporaneous birth control, eugenics and feminist ideologies. So the Hindu ancients may have proposed a lively coitus, but Britons at home were experiencing an unprecedented repression of sexual freedoms: a de facto ban on sexual education; a denunciation of masturbation as mentally scarring; and an assertion of all those aspects of prudery we find so easy to mock today – covered-up women's ankles and piano legs, for example.

By the time of Cunningham's expeditions, Britain had long forgotten the sexual exuberance that had held sway through the eighteenth and early nineteenth centuries, those years when men were celebrated for Byronic sexual potency; when London led the world trade in exports of pornographic pictorials; and when London brothels catered to every coital tastebud, from lovers of Japanese women to pederasts. As late as 1830, a nursing home in London looked after busy boy prostitutes afflicted with venereal disease. However, by the 1850s a vigorous moral campaign was being waged on British soil against prostitution, extra-conjugal sex, masturbation and sexual activity between males. In later decades, as we will explore, it would come to have far-reaching consequences for the subjects of that nation's colonial territories.

A century later, as Chapter 10 will show, the lustfulness of ancient Hinduism struck a chord with a generation of Westerners who were casting off the last vestiges of these late Victorian hang-ups. Inspired by the Western sexual revolution's prerogatives of chemical and sexual experimentation, these 'Goa Freaks' came to Khajuraho as part of a circuit that took in Kundalini-raising retreats in the Himalayas, the ghats at Varanasi and weeks-long LSD-fuelled sex orgies in pursuit of transcendence on Goan and Keralan beaches. The hippy set's attentions did much to create the haphazard tourist town that's now grown up at Khajuraho, little more than a backwater until the 1960s.

Today Khajuraho is firmly on the tourist map, for foreigners and inquisitive Indians alike. Even so, and as we'll also see in the pages to come, this shouldn't be taken as evidence that India has reached a greater ease with issues of sex and sexuality. As its economy forges ahead, social change – particularly around sex – is lagging behind. These attitudes are at the root of the headline-grabbing 2012 and 2013 Delhi gang rapes, and the uprisings that followed; and they're behind the daily miseries of life for many Indian women, who are routinely subject to being kidnapped for marriage and forced to wed against their will; being set light to when their dowries are considered insufficient by their groom; and raped within marriage with legal impunity (section 375 of the Indian Penal Code considers forced sex in marriage as a crime only when the wife is below the age of 15).

Further evidence of the incendiary response to sex and sexuality in today's India exists in the controversies around the modern counterparts to the sculptors at Khajuraho. M.F. Husain, India's most famous contemporary artist (and a Muslim), made his career on the scandal provoked by a series of paintings depicting copulating Hindu gods in flagrante (most famously Durga in sexual union with a tiger) while, more recently, an installation at Baroda's Maharaja Sayajirao University in Gujarat provoked uproar from religious groups for portraying sacred figures in naked poses, and led to the young artist's arrest and imprisonment.

Dimple and I have quite a ride ahead of us: from the heady heights of liberal Hinduism to the shadowy depths of Victorian repression. It's a road as rutted and variegated as the terrain we'll cross, from the hilly Himalayan north to the plains of the east; from the sultry south to the throbbing twenty-first-century metropolis of Bombay, on the western coast of the Arabian Sea. My eye alights on the auto's dashboard where, next to plastic Chinese flowers and a depiction of a many-armed Kali, hangs a keychain, much like the ones the hawkers were trying to sell us earlier. As we bounce up and down on the auto's clapped-out suspension, I watch in fascination as the keyring, featuring a mechanised miniature cock and vagina, thrusts suggestively in and out of itself, with an elegant staccato rhythm.

2 | THE RAGING RAJ, Shimla

The hill station of Shimla as a seat of sexual licence

Ours was a one-sexed society, with women hanging onto the edges... Some chased polo balls and some chased partridge. Some took up the most unlikely hobbies, and some went to diseased harlots... and some married in haste, only to worry over who was seducing their wives in the hill stations where they had seduced so many other people's wives.

—Lieutenant Colonel John Masters on life in the British Army in the 1930s

'It says here that it's a myth. The Victorians never dressed their indecent piano legs with little skirts,' I say.

Dimple and I are puffing uphill to the old hill station of Shimla on the Shivalik Deluxe. As Indian trains go, the Deluxe is luxurious: furnished with deep velvet cushioned seats and that more acquired taste, piped Hindi pop music. The train is celebrated by rail enthusiasts for what lies beneath us: a rare narrow-gauge rail track that was a feat of engineering in its day. It scissors through the sedimentary rocks of the Lower

Himalaya, across treetops and precipitous drops and 1500 feet of elevation, to the summer capital of the Raj.

I've caught the Deluxe a few times now and it's become my favourite train route among India's many. For the non-trainspotter, it's the view that gets you: every window filled with pine- and cedar-clad panoramas; and up ahead of us now, tumbling down the hillside like an illustration in a book of fairytales, the mock Tudor and Scottish baronial rooftops so characteristic of Shimla.

When we're not distracted by the view, we're reading up on the period in India's sexual history that we're here to explore. We'd started discussing the thesis for Shimla at Kalka railway station, amid the crush of bags and bodies that heralds every Indian train departure.

'The Victorians are every Briton's symbolic parents,' I'd informed Dimple. 'In a way, every British generation since has rebelled against their prudishness. So what I want to know is, is this the same for Indians?'

'They may be disapproving parents to you, but to Indians they're more like evil step-parents,' Dimple had replied, as we arrayed ourselves on padded seats, opposite a chattering Punjabi family. 'We love what the Britishers gave us in terms of democracy, cucumber sandwiches and English tailoring, but we hate what they took away from us: the labour of our people and our natural resources. So we're nostalgic about them in a way, but they're also the baddies. You can get a sense of that from Bollywood.'

She's right. From the 1960s on, the British became the stock baddies in Bollywood; like, perhaps, the Germans to Hollywood. The 1985 movie *Mard*, starring the demi-god of Bollywood, Amitabh Bachchan, is typical of the focus. In one scene, loosely based on the Jallianwala Bagh or Amritsar massacre of 1913 – when Brigadier-General Reginald E.H. Dyer ordered 50 Gurkha riflemen to fire into a crowd who'd assembled, in peaceful protest, in contravention of a British ban on public gatherings – an actor playing Lord Curzon, with a vainglorious glint in his eye, orders two mounted machine guns to open fire on the group of corralled 'natives'.

'The sexy piano/table legs thing,' I continue. 'Apparently it came from a parody of prudish Americans, written by a British naval man and novelist, Frederick Marryat.'

I'm reading from a webpage I'd downloaded when we last had a flicker of wi-fi access, back on the Kalka plains.

'That so?' says Dimple. 'I thought ankles were a big turn-on for the Britishers; that nice ladies didn't show them, and so on.'

'That was certainly true,' I continue, lowering my voice as a chai-wallah makes one of his 20 or so journeys up and down the carpeted aisle. He grimaces as he and his cargo are buffeted by air pressure when we enter the first of 104 tunnels we'll pass through during our five-hour journey up into the hills. 'Girls didn't show their ankles getting into carriages, or at least the boring girls didn't. In fact, even the word "legs" was thought to be too crude. The correct word was "limbs".'

'Good girls covered up their legs and bad boys got to wear metal chaddis?'

Dimple smirks. We'd just been poring over another internet quarry: a line drawing of the Stephenson Spermatic Truss. A metal hood dangling from a studded belt, this was a late nineteenth-century anti-masturbation device that permitted the wearer's penis to move freely until it became erect, whereupon its pressure against the metal hood would generate an electrical current.

The truss was one of around 30 anti-masturbation devices trademarked during the latter half of the British Empire, when the morally crusading Purity Campaigners were at their height. Masturbation – an act portrayed as a potential moral catastrophe and a cause of degeneration for the upcoming generation of upright empire builders – was one of their main targets. Dr William Acton, who wrote extensively on the subject, advised cold baths and quoits as prophylactics, though he schooled against horse riding. Inventors and entrepreneurs rushed into the field, offering everything from 'erection alarms' to anti-masturbation tonics.

Such devices, as well as other strange nineteenth-century exhibitions of sexual prudery, have since become cartoonishly synonymous in the West with the era we're here to explore: the Victorian and Edwardian age to the British, to Indians the Raj.

The Raj, British suzerainty over India, pertained for 90 years. It gave Britain the wealth that built its Victorian cities; it supplied its swagger and self-made men, as well as its tea, opium, saltpetre, cottons and silks. In return, it gave India its legal and bureaucratic framework, its sports and botanical gardens, and a railway system that remains the largest employer in the world.

Eventually, the British endeavour in India would carve off great hunks from the Indian subcontinent, provoking bloody communal massacres and inciting animosities that rumble on today, 60 years after India gained her independence. And Britain's intimate relationship with India would make its mark on both nations' sexual ethics – and sexual appetites.

Sexual dynamics underpinned the Victorian British Empire and its successful expansion. Indeed, the growth of the British Empire was as much powered by 'copulation and concubinage', as Cambridge historian Dr Ronald Hyam puts it, as it was by 'Christianity and commerce'.

For Victorians suffering a restriction of sexual freedoms at home, India's concubines, eunuchs and lotus-eyed ladies would prove unsettling and, for many, irresistible. In the early days of the twentieth century, the incidence of venereal disease among the army at home in Britain was 40 soldiers per 1000, whereas in India it was 110 per 1000. In 1887, a correspondent to the *Pall Mall Gazette* spoke for many when he bemoaned the tendency of colonial administrators to form 'immoral' relations in India, leaving their values back home 'along with Crosse and Blackwell's pickles or Keen's mustard'.

Back in Britain, the thirst for both a real and an imagined Oriental sensuality had taken hold. Despite newly toothy obscenity laws, Britain devoured India's literary erotica and, under its influence, would create oil-painted tableaux of harems and naked odalisques. For India, the racist undercurrents of the Raj would give shape to a character that already existed in Indian art and spiritual tradition: the white-skinned goddess, untouchable but, in the equivocal form of the colonial memsahib, also suddenly very much flesh and blood – ginger hair, freckles and all.

For British men stationed in India, the creation of the Empire provided exuberant possibilities for sexual experimentation. As another Cambridge historian, Roy Porter, put it, 'For many English travellers, exotic parts and peoples were realizations of fantasies, sources of sexual or mystical discovery, havens for scoundrels and screwballs, ways of jumping the rails of Western Classical-Christian Civilization.'

In Shimla, Dimple and I are staying at Wildflower Hall, a property that's now a luxury hotel, but was once the stately pile of a man who embodies Shimla's reputation for sexual heterodoxy: Herbert, First Earl Kitchener. In this fine alpine setting, Kitchener is remembered as the 'Jhungi Lat Sahib' or great warlord. He was the Commander-In-Chief of India from 1902 to 1909, though in the West he is most famous today as the army general behind the First World War enlistment campaign 'Your Country Needs You'.

Kitchener's delight in interior furnishing and horticulture, not least as seen at Wildflower Hall, led contemporary correspondents to comment 'It is an open secret that the commander-in-chief is an enthusiastic gardener', a phrase with a euphemistic flavour that resonates today.

In North Africa, as contemporary journalist Patrick Barkham put it, Kitchener had acquired the 'officer's failing... a taste for buggery'; and in Shimla, Kitchener maintained a habit from his days in Egypt of surrounding himself with an eager bunch of unmarried officers he nicknamed 'Kitchener's happy band of boys'.

Another take on his sexual taste comes from historian A.N. Wilson. 'When the great field marshal stayed in aristocratic houses,' Wilson said in the 2009 BBC documentary *The Victorians*, 'the well-informed young would ask servants to sleep across their bedroom threshold to impede his entrance. Kitchener's compulsive objective was sodomy, irrespective of gender.'

Kitchener also had no use for married men on his staff, cultivated a great interest in Robert Baden-Powell's Boy Scout moment, avoided interviews with women wherever possible and decorated his rose garden at Shimla with bronze sculptures of naked boys.

Other historians suggest that Kitchener's passion for boys – pederasty in contemporary parlance – was unconsummated, his pleasure coming chiefly from 'scopophilia' or the act of gazing at the young, naked male form. In Kitchener's time, such interests were far from marginal. Until the 1930s, popular culture continued to support a strong emotional interest in young boys. Artistically suspect 'Uranian poets' flourished throughout the Edwardian period, conjuring purple stanzas celebrating 'splendid strapping boys' and 'forbidden lips'. And male-oriented men, as we'll see later, soon found an outlet on Indian soil.

Kitchener wasn't the only one up to mischief in Shimla's foothills; far from it. From the earliest days of its position as the summer capital of the Raj, it became a place for British men, including convalescing and holidaying soldiers, to enjoy a spot of restorative 'jiggy-jig', and one where the sexual ethics in operation on the Indian plains, and certainly back home in Britain, were temporarily suspended.

In 1890, Diwan Jeewan Das, Minister of the Raja of Kapurthala, summed up the atmosphere at Shimla as most people saw it: a place where 'gaiety, frivolity and sex indulgence' reigned. That was a far cry from the public morality of buttoned-up, pinned-down Victorian Britain.

The following morning, Dimple and I are bouncing downhill on the back seat of an Ambassador cab. We're with Raaja Chopra, a historian who's spent his career researching the larger-than-life characters who peopled Shimla during its 80 years as the Raj summer capital. Raaja has arranged for us to be dropped at the lower edge of town, at Cart Road, to take in a little of the atmosphere of Shimla present, as we consider the excesses of Shimla past. Today it's Karva Chauth, a festival in which local women fast through daylight hours for the well-being of their sons, fiancés and husbands, so the city's zigzagging alleyways are packed.

From the veg carts and taxi stands of Cart Road, it's a lively 20-minute walk, via a warren of bazaars, to the Ridge, the focal point of this hillside city since the days of the Raj. A hawker pushes a platter of milk-based sweets under our noses, and Dimple sniffs luxuriantly.

'The bazaar has followed this layout since the early Britishers were here, so the atmosphere would have been much the same,' says Raaja. 'But then they were selling perfumes from Paris, silk gloves and tropical corsets, too; and the shoppers would probably be on jampans, on an Indian's shoulders. This was a boomtown, you have to remember. A fifth of the word's population was ruled through Shimla's two telegraph wires – a fifth!'

The hawkers are doing a brisk trade in bangles, ribbons and votive candies. 'Tonight women will exchange gifts and dress up in bright sarees and shalwars,' Raaja explains. 'As I see it, Karva Chauth is as much about the women treating themselves as a gesture to the town's menfolk.'

We're here to find out about another group of spunky women associated with Shimla. In its British Indian heyday, the city was awash all summer long with the cream of British Indian society in pursuit of their frivolities and indulgences, but one societal subgroup became more notorious than most.

'The Grass Widows were wives of Raj officials who were spending the summer in Shimla while their husbands remained on the plains.' Raaja continues the conversation we'd started in the cab. 'Grass was probably a reference to the fresher mountain air. These women were famous for their sexual escapades. They earned themselves nicknames: the "Charpoy Cobra", charpoy being a traditional woven bed; the "Subaltern's Guide", named for her taste for subalterns or junior officers; the "Bed-and-Breakfast", who explains herself; and my own personal favourite, the "Passionate Haystack".'

The idea of the predatory older woman first arrived in modern popular Western culture in the 1967 movie *The Graduate*, in which rudderless university graduate Kevin Braddock (played by Dustin Hoffman) is famously seduced by bored older housewife Mrs Robinson (played by Anne Bancroft). In that common celluloid distortion, Bancroft was in fact only six years Hoffman's senior. Perhaps it was because the romantic pairing of a powerful older woman and a subordinate younger man in a climate in which fewer than 40 per cent of women participated in the labour force was rare, but there was a marked lack of judgemental comment on Mrs Robinson's motivations.

By the twenty-first century, however, the predatory older woman was not considered so innocuous, picking up her notorious feline alias the 'cougar', as well as a tougher edge. In American television depictions, such as *Desperate Housewives* and the Courtney Cox vehicle *Cougar Town*, she's a plastic predator, cosmetically improved to within an inch of her eyebrow line, and the arch consumer of both luxury footwear and men. Bloodlusty, but somehow bloodless, in many ways she's the daughter of that stock 1980s figure, the power-dressing businesswoman.

'Not everyone was happy about these predatory older women during the Raj,' continues Raaja. 'I have something here that will give you an idea.' With this, he pulls us away from the crowds, into an alcove next to a hole-in-the-wall bangle store. He extracts a small wad of papers from his belted suit trousers.

It's a 1913 cutting about the Grass Widows from a local publication, lampooning the 'seasoned spinsters and speculating mammas', and the latters' complaint that the Grass Widows are 'collecting and enticing away all the eligible bachelors from the unmarried generation'.

'So there was less a moral complaint about the Grass Widows' antics, more one claiming territorial rights over unmarried men?' I ask Raaja, the insight surprising me.

'That's right,' he replies, 'and we see the tension elsewhere in society too. Look at this, a Rudyard Kipling poem, "My Rival". It was written in 1885, by which point Kipling had spent many summers in Shimla and had seen these antics at first hand. The poem's the lament of a Fishing Fleet girl, a

British woman who'd come to India in search of a husband, that the older Grass Widows are ruining her chances with Shimla's eligible bachelors.'

The young men come, the young men go
Each pink and white and neat,
She's older than their mothers,
But they grovel at Her feet.
They walk beside Her 'rickshaw wheels –
None ever walk by mine;
And that's because I'm seventeen
And She is forty-nine.

I wish I had Her constant cheek;
I wish that I could sing
All sorts of funny little songs,
Not quite the proper thing.
I'm very gauche and very shy,
Her jokes aren't in my line;
And, worst of all, I'm seventeen
While She is forty-nine.

'You know, there was another thing,' adds Raaja, neatly folding his sheath of cuttings. 'Sex with a Grass Widow could be a career move for a young captain. There was a clear relationship between being spotted – perhaps as a handsome young officer playing amateur dramatics on the stage at the Shimla Gaiety Theatre – and achieving preferment and promotion. Numerous young men were skilled in manipulating bored women to their advantage in this way. They were nicknamed poodle-fakers, poodle being slang for a silly woman.'

Sex is the oldest route to preferment, of course. The Kama Sutra emphasises married women with powerful husbands as an appropriate subject for a citizen's sexual attentions:

> *The woman has gained the heart of her great and powerful husband, and exercises a mastery over him, who is a friend of my enemy; if, therefore, she becomes united with me, she will cause her husband to abandon my enemy. (Burton translation, 1883)*

We settle down over white tablecloths, scones and tea in the vaulted tearoom of one of the heritage hotels that anchor the Mall. Around us, well-fed European, Indian and American tourists clink heavy silver tableware and chat reverently or uproariously according to national stereotype. The property is now owned by a five-star brand that made its fortune, so the gossip goes, supplying beds by the hour to Raj soldiers and prostitutes in early twentieth-century Calcutta.

Dimple sets about introducing spoon after spoon of white sugar to the pale gold depths of her teacup. We've gone for a high-quality Darjeeling, which, Raaja had promised, with the impromptu poetry of the educated Indian, would be 'like the Himalayan sunlight at dawn'.

'The Fishing Fleets are my favourites among the characters of old Shimla,' he says, returning to our theme. 'In the early days there were few takers for the rigours of the colonial lifestyle, so the East India Company, the trading company that preceded British crown governance of India, made it worth these girls' while. They paid their passage out, gave them a set of clothing, and maintained them for a year.

'But by the late nineteenth century the tables had turned. India, where there were four white women to every one white man, was seen as the last-ditch hunting ground for British women not sufficiently pretty or rich to make a good match at home. So the Company started charging a £200 bond – equivalent to £12,000 today – to girls who wanted to make the trip.'

'God, it's like a spinster tax,' I say.

'You're not joking,' adds Dimple, nodding into her steaming cup.

'But there was no shortage of willing Fishing Fleet girls,' says Raaja. 'By this point they also had the Highway to India, which was what they called the Suez Canal back then. It opened to non-shipping traffic in 1869 and reduced the average journey time from England to India from six months to around six weeks. So the floodgates opened, if you will. The cargo of young damsels became an annual event.'

'And these girls hot-footed it to Shimla to find husbands?' I ask.

'The more business-minded girls, those who wanted a good husband at any cost, might get themselves affianced on the boat trip. Others were snapped up at the port in Bombay by the desperate, undersexed men who awaited their arrival: for them it must have been like a cargo of exotic fruits and they wanted first pick of the produce.

'But yes, many girls came directly to Shimla for the summer season, with their chaperones or "speculating mammas" and their trunks of evening dresses. By the early twentieth century, a trip here had become the British debutante's rite of passage.'

'And if they didn't find a husband?' asks Dimple.

Raaja smiles as he smothers his scone with butter. 'I'm afraid it would be social suicide: those who went back to England without a marriage band, or at least an engagement ring, were called "Returned Empties".'

I think of the mixture of excitement and desperation that must have drawn many of these girls across these turbulent seas – the much-feared waters of the Bay of Biscay and the 'pirate alley' of the Red Sea – to seek a mate.

The nineteenth century was manifestly cruel to the unmarried middle-class woman. Without a husband, she'd suffer a lack of social status; and without a man's or her own independent income, she'd be thrown on the mercy of her relatives. Or she might suffer an icier fate still as a governess: a lonely figure with no rightful place, or companionship, above or below stairs.

It was the emphasis on keeping up with the Joneses that was partly to blame for this glut of unmarried girls, or what became known as the 'spinster issue'. For a middle-class Victorian man, marriage came not only with the expense of keeping a large family property and a wife, but also that of maintaining their numerous offspring and the retinue of servants expected of a polite home. Understandably, many men eyed this fate warily and decided against marriage, preferring to live a bachelor life in cheaper lodgings while relying on prostitutes to cater to their earthier needs. The number of working girls on the streets of Victorian London – one for every 12 adult males – indicates the popularity of this life choice.

'High stakes for these Fishing Fleet girls, then?' I ask.

'Yes,' agrees Raaja. 'There was a lot riding on their hooking a man. And apart from their competition with the Grass Widows, other factors were working against them at Shimla. Their potential haul was severely reduced by the army's disapproval of early marriage. An unmarried soldiery was believed to be more efficient, so the Indian Army rule of thumb was 'subalterns cannot marry; captains may marry; majors should marry; colonels must marry'. Trouble was, men were usually in their early to mid-30s before they were promoted to the status of officer, so most of the younger men were selected out of the marriage market by circumstance.

'Shimla society could be quite cruel towards these girls, too,' he went on. 'Wits had a lot of fun with the phenomenon. One contemporary snidely described the arrival of the Fishing Fleets as a "matrimonial armada hoving into view".

They were also given cruel nicknames. Three unattractive sisters who came to Shimla were known as "The World, the Flesh and the Devil", and another three became "Wriggles, Giggles and Goggles".'

Perhaps the modern-day equivalent of these breathless matrimonial armadas can be seen in Western cities such as New York. In 2005, Columbia University economist Lena Edlund ran a study into the single male to single female ratios across major world cities and came up with some startling results. In 44 of the 47 cities she studied, women outnumbered men (in the remaining three cities there was parity). The shortage of available males was particularly acute in New York (and increased substantially in the 1990s), as picked up in pithy monologue by that notorious New York single girl, *Sex and the City*'s Carrie Bradshaw (although Carrie's numbers are slightly off, including, as they do, New York octogenarians): 'There are 1.3 million single men in New York, 1.8 million single women, and of these more than 3 million people, about 12 think they're having enough sex.'

Edlund's paper, also called 'Sex and the City', proposes 'that such a pattern may be linked to higher male incomes in urban areas; the presence of males with high incomes attracting not only skilled females but also unskilled females. Thus, a surplus of women in urban areas may result from a combination of better labor and marriage markets.' In short, when big-city rents rise in the West, lower-earning males leave for smaller towns while their lower-earning female counterparts cling on – in a tactic not dissimilar to that of the Fleet girls, the potential of a rich mate as their prize.

In an analysis of Edlund's findings, Tim Harford, in his book *The Logic of Life*, speculates that rather than causing women a modest inconvenience, 'this tiny imbalance ends up being very bad news for the women, and very good news for the remaining men. Scarcity is power; and more power than you might have thought.' With a surplus of available women, men have little or no incentive to marry, leading to fractious and neurotic competition for male attention. As one single 39-year-old New York woman once summed it up to me: 'It's a candy store for these guys. Men are like taxi cabs: women get in, women get out. When the light goes on they're ready to marry, when the lights are off – no chance.'

There are, of course, two main key differences between the tough marital economy faced by today's New York singletons and that of the unmarried girls of Victorian Britain: economic independence, and sexual freedom.

'I bet Giggles was expected to be innocent to the ways of the flesh until her wedding night,' I suggest.

'She'd have to be very careful to preserve her reputation, yes,' says Raaja.

'Good Indian Girls, Good English Girls... It's the same old story for young women in conservative times,' says Dimple.

'Yes,' I agree with a smile, draining my cup of Himalayan sunlight as we pack up for the walk back through the still buzzing bazaar. 'But what if you get to be a Grass Widow when you grow up?'

3 | BLACK ON WHITE, Shimla

Sex, race and the bad-boy Maharajas

The issues Miss Quested had raised were so much more important than she was herself that people inevitably forgot her.

—*E.M. Forster,* A Passage to India

If sex was titillation, or a career move, for the well-heeled British of Shimla society, it was something very different for Rajeev Kuthiala's relatives. Now in his late 80s, Kuthiala remembers the Raj caravan through his eyes as a young boy in the 1920s and 1930s.

Raaja, Dimple and I have arranged to meet him the next morning at Scandal Point. A smooth sweep of concrete where the Mall broadens across the Ridge, Scandal Point is today what it was then: the natural spot for Shimlaites to meet friends and lovers, promenade in their finery and exchange gossip. As so frequently in Shimla, the air smells impossibly fresh, the sky's as blue as lapis lazuli and the flora is putting on its best show: everywhere at the roadside the Rhododendron varietal the Shimlaites call buransh is in full mid-red bloom, its cluster of buds gaping like the serried mouths of trumpets.

Kuthiala arrives with his patient great-niece Geeta, who's walked him up the hill to meet us. As she coaxes him to lean on her arm for support, the old man bashes his stick on the concrete underfoot in noisy irritation.

From the age of 14, Kuthiala was a hand rickshaw puller, as was his father before him and his father before that. First in line was his great-grandfather, who was press-ganged into service as a coolie from his hillside village in the 1860s. In those days the hill roads were impassable to wheeled vehicles, so all the gaudy brocade of the Raj was borne up here on Indian backs: chests of tea, boxes of files, houseplants and pets, even costumes for am-dram at the Gaiety.

There was certainly no shortage of servants to supply British needs. In a typical Shimla Summer Census, that from 1921, the city was home to 43,333 souls, of whom 4803 were Europeans and 38,503 were their Indian servants or dependants: shopkeepers and ayahs (maids and coolies), with one rickshaw puller, such as Kuthiala, for every white head.

But Shimla's sexual permissiveness represented a complication, rather than a pleasure, for Kuthiala's servant family. His second uncle was, he says, the fruit of his grandmother's liaison with a white man; an incident that his grandmother claimed, on the rare occasions she could be prevailed upon to talk about her life, was rape. She was married at the time to Kuthiala's grandfather and the family lived on the outskirts of town.

'He says it was rarely talked about in his family,' says Raaja, who's carefully translating Kuthiala's mixture of Hindi and Punjabi. 'The child was brought up by his great-aunt in the village so as not to attract scandal. His grandfather grew to despise his wife and became a drunk on zutho, the local moonshine. There was no money from the father or acknowledgement of the child.'

'So he remembers the wild ways of the British?' I ask.

'Yes,' says Raaja, after a pause to translate. 'He says they feared for the young girls of their family. The Britisher men were notorious, and his sister was sent back to the family village so she wouldn't be corrupted. He says that village girls could be ruined if they fell in with a Britisher man.'

Even back in England at the height of Victorian repression, sex with servants was the norm. The great psychoanalyst Sigmund Freud was far from unusual in losing his virginity to a scullery maid. Household servants were easy to access for lusty boys, often literally – knickers only came into use for the British working classes in the 1850s. And in India, there was the added factor of the 'Oriental' attraction felt by many Victorian males.

In the early days of the East India Company, it was tacitly accepted that white men in India would take Indian women for their wives, or bibis. Originally a Hindustani word denoting a high-class woman, in Anglo-Indian usage the term bibi came to connote a native mistress.

Job Charnock (1630–92), the colourful East India Company administrator who founded Calcutta at the site of Sutanati, a small town beside the Hoogly river, sired three children by the Hindu bibi he saved from sati, the ritual self-immolation rite whereby widows throw themselves on their husbands' funeral pyres in tribute to that perfect mythological wife Sita. Meanwhile, Colonel James Skinner had a harem of 14 wives with whom he reputedly fathered 80 children. Further down the social scale, many of the British in India during the Company days married Hindu women, or preferably Anglo-Indians (those with mixed European/Indian parentage, then called Eurasians). Indeed, in the late eighteenth century the East India Company actively encouraged such liaisons, paying five rupees for every Eurasian child of a rank soldier who was baptised.

Common as these interracial sexual set-ups may have been, they were also necessarily unequal. Bibis existed in a precarious position between spouse, companion and prostitute. They were recruited through servants and would draw a salary for their time with their 'master', which often spanned several years. Any children issuing from the relationship would be housed, fed and schooled. The luckier bibis inherited estates, although few were accorded the respect that white wives enjoyed. Bibis were routinely barred from attending functions as their master's companion. And when their men wearied of them, many Indian mistresses would be left to destitution, separated from their children, who remained the legal property of their master. For Indian women in the eighteenth and nineteenth centuries – and for Kuthiala's grandmother – mating with a European man, whether voluntarily or under coercion, could spell ruin.

Yet it was also true that bibis could become adept at holding their masters in their emotional and sexual thrall. The diaries of Calcutta surveyor and architect Richard Blechynden, written between 1791 and 1822, portray how emotionally muddy these entanglements could become. In April 1800, the diaries report a month of sleepless misery after his bibi Mary left him for a Captain James:

> *Not one minute's sleep did I obtain… This woman will drive me mad I believe. Reason tells me that it is a happy riddance – but passion oversetts [sic] the whole of that and I return to my regret for having let her go.*

Back home, these Anglo-Indian arrangements were often viewed with distaste, even in the early years. Blechynden tells of a passionate letter written to a young Calcutta lieutenant of his acquaintance from the lieutenant's father, the Reverend Hastings, against the immorality of keeping an

Indian girl and siring two children by her. William was, his father arraigned, 'living in a pagan country where this view of fornication is allowed, and encouraged, by the natives, and is eagerly copied and practiced by their European infidel masters'.

In the late eighteenth century, compounded by the colonial uprisings of 1791 on the Caribbean island of Santo Domingo where whites were rounded up and massacred, these relatively open attitudes towards Indian mistresses went into an abrupt reverse. In 1773, the Regulating Act had created the post of Governor General of Bengal with administrative powers over all of British India. In 1786, when Lord Cornwallis assumed the post, he brought in a programme of edicts that would result in an impassable barrier – social, sexual and economic – between British and Indians. The first banned the children of British men and Indian women from jobs within the Company. The second forbade such mixed-race children from being sent home to England to be educated, and determined that no one with an Indian parent could be employed in the civil, military or marine branches of the Company. These laws, in effect, made formal intermarriage untenable.

Another form of interracial union – the white female and the Indian male – was also deeply problematic. Scandal Point, where we're standing, is named for one of these supposed interracial liaisons: the elopement of the daughter of British India's top official, the Viceroy, and a dashing Indian prince.

'There were nubile Viceroy's daughters around this period, of course,' says Raaja, as he explains this story. 'But there's little historical evidence that the Scandal Point events actually happened, or that the individuals in question even existed.'

The urban legend of Scandal Point hints at something that was indubitably true, though: a deep-seated fear, by the time of Raj-era India, of sexual relations between white females and non-white males. It was a fear that was lampooned in E.M. Forster's 1924 novel *A Passage to India*, in which a young Indian Muslim physician, Aziz, is mistakenly arrested for sexually assaulting young British schoolmistress Adela Quested. The novel plays with the tensions between whites and Indians in the run-up to the Indian Independence movement, expressed in a societal neurosis around interracial coupling.

The inflection point had come after the events of the Indian Rebellion of 1857, known as 'India's First War of Independence' to Indians and as the 'Sepoy Mutiny' to the British. While incidents of war rape committed by Indian rebels against English women and girls did occur, these were exaggerated to great effect by the British media in order to justify vicious reprisals and the continuance of colonialism.

The propaganda reached fever pitch in the 1860s, when the British press in India argued that Indian judges were abusing their powers to fill their harems with white English females. In the wake of the Indian Rebellion, 'sexual pollution' and the degeneration of the white race via miscegenation came to be directly linked with social chaos and the fall of Empire. The Industrial Revolution, too, expanded the social chasm between black and white, encouraging the British belief in their mastery and superiority – their distinctness from the 'black races'. Indeed, many British viewed their successes in heavy industry and engineering as indicative of their natural right to rule over their less technologically advanced subject peoples.

The motif of the 'dark-skinned rapist' began to proliferate in nineteenth-century English literature. In the days leading up to the massacre at Amritsar on April 13, 1919, Indian men were required to crawl on their stomachs, hands and knees at the sight of a white woman, following an attack on an

English missionary, Miss Marcella Sherwood, which obviously inspired Forster's narrative. General Dyer, who issued the order, later explained to a British inspector:

> *Some Indians crawl face downwards in front of their gods. I wanted them to know that a British woman is as sacred as a Hindu god and therefore they have to crawl in front of her, too.*

Despite this unbridled paranoia, there remained an attraction between Indian males and white women. The sisters of the unmarried Lord Auckland (Viceroy 1836–42), who were his hostesses, raised eyebrows at Shimla with the consistent good looks of their young, male (and Indian) aides-de-camp. And interracial love affairs between Indian men and white women did occur, Raaja tells us as we watch Kuthiala retreating slowly back down the hill, dyspeptically shooing away his great-niece's arm.

'For a while the maharajas had special dispensation in this respect,' Raaja explains. 'The early twentieth century was considered to be their golden era and a new generation of ultra-sophisticated and jet-setting Maharajas took the world by storm. They hobnobbed with the British royal family, movie stars, glamorous models and European aristocrats.

'And at Shimla, these Indian royals were very much in pursuit of English roses. There was one particularly notorious group of bad-boy princes: Rajinder Singh of Patiala; Jagatjit Singh Bahadur, Maharaja of Kapurthala; and the Raja of Dholpu. Handsome, pampered Sikhs, they would stroll about town in pink turbans, thigh-high black leather boots and strings of pearls and emeralds. For their sport, along with the hunts and gymkhanas, they seduced English girls. And they did this,' Raaja says with a grin, 'by going for every Englishwoman's Achilles' heel.'

For a pleasurable moment, I wonder what this enticement might be. Tea leaves, perhaps, or a year's supply of crumpets?

'They loaned the girls horses to soften their will,' he went on. 'The only thoroughbreds to be had at the time were in the Maharanis' stables, you see. Otherwise there were the temperamental Indian packhorses, which made for poor riding. So the Maharajas would loan horses to the girls and demand a dinner date from them in return. It was a successful tactic, and their love games with English girls were apparently tolerated because of their royal status. Nevertheless, they were playing a game as dangerous as the girls, because racism was very real in the latter days of the Raj. And, of course, they overstepped the mark...'

'What happened?' asks Dimple.

'Well,' continues Raaja, 'there was an incident in 1903 when the then Viceroy, Lord Curzon, was out of town. He was a bit of a stick-in-the-mud who viewed Shimla's social scene with distaste. After several homosexual experiences as a student at Eton, including kissing a male teacher, Curzon had ruthlessly rejected romance in pursuit of his career development, and in his tenure as Viceroy had argued forcibly for aloofness between races. He failed, despite enthusiastic attempts, to stop the marriage of the Maharaja of Patiala to one Miss Florry Bryan, and the Maharaja of Jind wed a Dutch woman in secret to escape Curzon's attentions. The Viceroy also blocked the Raja of Pudukkottai from attending Queen Victoria's funeral in London in 1901, believing he was scouting for a white bride.

'So our princes were taking a risk when they invited his beautiful wife, American heiress Lady Mary Victoria Curzon, to one of the Maharaja of Patiala's three palaces to view his family jewels. Here, by all accounts, she got a bit giddy and played dress-up in royal sarees as well as the star in his collection: a tiara containing a 52-carat brilliant that Napoleon had given as a wedding gift to Empress Eugenie de Montijo in 1853 – the famous Eugenie diamond.'

'How did Curzon find out?' asks Dimple.

'Now, that really was bad luck,' continues Raaja. 'A photography pioneer, Lala Deen Dayal, was a guest at the palace and he snapped a picture of Lady Mary. A few weeks later, the shots somehow surfaced in the British newspapers. Lord Curzon hit the roof, of course, and our bad boys were banned from Shimla town. For the Maharajas and their English roses, the party was over.'

Later that evening, Dimple and I are sitting on the terrace of Wildflower Hall, digesting the day over a G&T: that drink so defining of the Raj, invented to convince British-Indian soldiers to ingest their anti-malarial quinine. It always tastes better in India, somehow, as martinis do after nightfall on New York's Upper Eastside, or Campari *aperitivos* in early-evening Milan.

I ask Dimple if Shimla has given her a new take on the British in India.

'I still think the Britishers were racist, sexist and hypocritical,' she says, after a moment's thought. 'But I don't think they were quite as repressed as their reputation.'

Even at the height of the Purity Movement, the Victorian world had its sex rebels – those we've glimpsed in Shimla's Grass Widows and disporting officers, and also those back home. In London there was a lively cruising scene for male–male anonymous sex, and it was the service menus of Victorian London brothels, rather than American GIs as is commonly believed, that gave us the term 'blow job' (an abbreviation for 'below job').

There were also numerous flagellation establishments in Victorian London, though perhaps this sexual peccadillo for pain, contemporaneously known as 'the English vice', is less exclusively English than we think. The Kama Sutra devotes a chapter to the arts of 'Pressing or Marking or Scratching with the Nails', another largely to 'Biting' and another to 'the various Ways of Striking and of the Sounds appropriate to them'.

'There's something else I read on the way up here,' I say to Dimple, who's watching the muscular forms of the Himalayas darken as the night stealthily claims the day. The sound of macaque monkey calls bounces across the hillsides, like hysterical human laughter.

'About Queen Victoria,' I say. 'Apparently she used to hammer on Albert's bedroom door demanding her conjugal rights in German: *"Diese Tür zu öffnen! Ich bin die Königin"* (Open this door! I am the Queen).'

Dimple laughs, dribbling G&T down her chin. 'No wonder Albert had to put a staple through it!'

PART TWO: THE NORTH II

And how it feels now

Bodybuilding shop, Amritsar (Sally Howard)

4 | ALL ABOUT EVE-TEASING, Delhi

Feminists tire of roaming hands – and anti-groping flash mobs on the metro

[Pursuit of] pleasures can lead a man into distress, and into contact with low persons; they cause him to commit unrighteous deeds, and produce impurity in him; they make him regardless of the future, and encourage carelessness and levity.

—Kama Sutra, Burton translation, 1883

It occurred to me as I planned for this trip that, when it comes to the petty sexual molestations I've experienced, I never count India. I think of the Greek speedboat owner who thrust my hand down his tight white shorts when I was 15; or the man on the New York subway who pressed his erection against me when, naively, I thought he was nudging me with an overstuffed holdall. But I never count India. After all, ISPs, or Indian Sex Pests, are par for the course for the white woman travelling in India; as are the Weekend Crotch Watchers who gather to ogle white women in bikinis on Goa's beaches.

When I once complained about the regularity of my encounters with roaming Indian hands, Dimple suggested to me that it was all the fault of Britney Spears.

'What are Indian boys to do when they see the white goddess and she's pulled off her pedestal?' she said. 'There's the white goddess, who's a pure untouchable beauty; you see her in iconography all over India. And you see the white-faced girl, in the adverts for Fair & Lovely cream, as the goody-goody pure girl. But then you have this tsunami of sexy white girls in American movies and pop videos, thrusting and grinding, openly having sex. And there she is, too, wearing a bikini on the beach in Goa, while all the Indian tourists cover up. No wonder that to most Indian boys, being white is a sign you're sexually available.'

'And therefore up for it with any passing man or boy?' I'd responded, shaking my head. 'Ugh, I've definitely come across that attitude.'

The many Indian groping incidents I'd heard of, involving friends and friends' girlfriends, were often surreally impressive. The young man, for example, who'd cycled alongside two female friends in their moving train carriage, keeping pace while masturbating; the young boy who'd brought himself to climax while chatting to a blonde friend over the wall of her Goan villa; or the autorickshaw driver who'd distracted a friend's boyfriend by pointing at the horizon, so he could hoot her breasts like car horns.

Traditionally these attentions – groping to Westerners, eve-teasing to Indians – were seen as nothing more than a monumental pain in the ass. Increasingly, however, they're becoming viewed as something more serious. Such incidents are fast losing their slap-and-tickle innocuousness, following a wave of violent and increasingly publicized sexual attacks across India, but most brutally in Delhi, India's crowded capital city to which Dimple and I are now travelling by train – a city on the front line of the clash between Indian social attitudes, ancient and modern.

'Positionssss!' Sweetie hisses at my shoulder. It's a late autumn day in New Delhi and I'm here, so hot beneath two layers of T-shirt that my palm is leaving damp hand prints against the chromium-plated handrail of the Metro's Violet Line. We're travelling at speed southeast from the interchange of Central Secretariat towards the well-heeled Delhi suburbs: Kailash Colony, and South Extensions One and Two, where the Indian middle classes are busy buying slabs of imported manchego for 200 rupees a pop before haggling over their 20-rupee rickshaw ride home.

Running parallel to us, and sometimes above, there's an older Delhi: one of bleating horns, busted pavements and that custard smog of precipitation that's the annual side effect – despite the Indian Central Government's blustery campaigns – of the Diwali firecracker season. And here I am, a white woman in a carriage stocked with silent, middle-class Indian male commuters, clutching an 18-rupee ticket for a ride on that sleek incarnation of India's twenty-first-century ambition: the New Delhi Metro. And I'm not particularly prepared for this gig.

'Arrrrgh. Bas, you lecher!'

'Aaiyo... what happen to you baby? Did you get hurt?'

From somewhere near to the rubber concertina that delineates the open border between the train's General and Ladies Only compartments, a female voice emits a yelp.

'Mujhe touch mat karo! Get your gande hands off me! Can't you men see that this is the Ladies' Compartment? Don't you have any mothers and sisters?'

Until now, and in contrast to the brooding atmosphere in the General car, Ladies Only has bubbled with activity: knots of women in sarees gossiping; blue jeans-wearing teens prodding their mobiles; students mouthing into open text-books. Now they, too, become still. All the activity is around the woman with the rising decibels, who's imploring men in neighbouring seats: 'Bachao! This badmash is troubling me.'

A businessman with a moustache that makes it look as if he's peering over a privet hedge buries his head in the *Economic Times of India*. Next to him, a small Bengali man stops looking out the window and, disinterestedly, pipes up, 'Calm yourself, calm yourself madam. Here, take my seat, madam; calm yourself.'

'I'm not moving,' mutters a man who's among the ten or so males who've inched into the steel-box gynaeceum of Ladies Only.

Now, on the signal of Sweetie's raised arm, five of us – three women, two men – scattered at points along the con-joined carriages, step forward like air stewards heralding a safety announcement. A silent count of 'one, two, three' and we peel off our top T-shirts to reveal what's below: match-ing canary-yellow T-shirts bearing, in blocky black type, the slogan 'Main Cheez Nahin Hun Mast Mast'.

A lyric from a song-and-dance number in a popular Bollywood movie, 'Main Cheez Nahin Hun Mast Mast', or 'I am not an item', is a pun on that genre's 'item' or sexy cameo dancing girls. The twist was the idea of Rosalyn D'mello, the Goan-born activist behind direct action organisation Mind the Gap – and it's Mind the Gap that is behind the event I am attend-ing, one of a number of anti-eve-teasing flash mobs staged intermittently on the New Delhi Metro.

Anti-eve-teasing meme (Aishik Saha)

D'mello hatched the plan for her first flash mob in 2011 after her friend Sushila experienced a textbook eve-teasing incident. Travelling home from a teaching shift at night class in Central Delhi, Sushila was slapped by a male Metro passenger, before having her breasts opportunistically groped in the kerfuffle that ensued.

'Indian women are standing up,' D'mello had told me when we met in a smart bookstore-cum-café in Delhi's middle-class shopping district, Khan Market. Drinking buffalo-milk cappuccinos and eating masala-laced quiche to the sound of car horns from Subramaniam Bharti Marg – a thoroughfare named for a nineteenth-century Tamil activist who campaigned for the emancipation of Indian women and the lower castes – D'mello had complained: 'Delhi has a culture of casual sexual harassment of women, and yet ministers have issued press releases saying it's the fault of women; that wearing jeans unleashes men's "animal passions"; that women shouldn't go out after 2 a.m. if we don't want to invite rape. Huh! As if the streets are safe at 1.30 a.m.!'

Covering anything from cat-calling to petty groping and chher chaar (the making of a sexual pass at a woman), eve-teasing fascinates English-speaking visitors to India. Why Eve and not, say, Sita? And why the lightheartedness the nickname implies? Are Indian women – unlike their Western counterparts – generally relaxed about roving hands and eyes?

Eve-teasing has a religious seal of approval, too. The god Krishna, an old roué held to have a thousand wives, is described as having a weakness for eve-teasing cowherding girls, especially his beloved Radha. It's Krishna's appetite for eve-teasing that's celebrated in the springtime festival of Holi, when young Indian men are given de facto permission to grope young girls as they douse them with water and dust them with coloured powder in the traditional 'Holi play'.

Holi play reaches its apogee at the small medieval town of Barsana in Uttar Pradesh (a large, populous state to the immediate south of Delhi), which has one of the few temples dedicated to Radha. At Lath Mar Holi, a festival at Barsana that takes place a few days before Holi proper, town women beat up men with sticks in retaliation against the indiscretions of Krishna; an event all the more powerful for the fact that the villagers dose themselves in preparation on thandhi, a milk drink laced with cannabis paste.

Silsila, a 1981 Bollywood movie starring Amitabh Bachchan, is typical of many pop-cultural depictions of Holi as an opportunity for the fairer sex to submit, coquettishly, to a spot of eve-teasing. In the plot, struggling writer Amit (Bachchan) woos Chandi (screen siren Rekha) with a plate of Holi sweetmeats and his wandering hands. Meanwhile, Chandi breathily rebuts him, bosom heaving in a hint of arousal/submission.

Such notions of coercive wooing were not always the case in India, however. The Kama Sutra advises the man about town to woo his chosen girl skilfully, at first 'in a lonely place with soft words' instilling confidence, rather than to break down resistance via a battering ram of manly force. Indeed, Vatsayana counsels against such a brutish technique:

> *A girl forcibly enjoyed by one who does not understand the hearts of girls becomes nervous, uneasy and dejected, and suddenly begins to hate the man who has taken advantage of her; and then, when her love is not understood or returned, she sinks into despondency and becomes either a hater of mankind altogether or, hating her own man, she has recourse to other men.*

As far as D'mello is concerned, such blithe depictions of eve-teasing – as a game in which young women are part complicit – are dangerous. To her generation of young Indian women (and their male sympathisers), eve-teasing has become the symbol of everything that's distorted in the Indian attitude to women and sex: the first rung on a ladder that ends in eye-popping rates of rape, dowry death and domestic violence.

And she's not wrong about the violence. As of 2010, according to a *Times of India* study, 60 per cent of married Indian women were suffering some form of domestic abuse. A January 2012 article in news weekly *India Today*, headed 'Hatya Shastra: the new face of domestic murder', sensationally discussed India's 'epidemic' of domestic murders:

> *Across urban India, bedrooms have become dangerous arenas of war, not love. The enemy is within, waiting to strike. In Bangalore, Kumar, a 27-year-old garment worker, hit his pregnant wife in a fit of anger*

> *for demanding new clothes on New Year. The blow killed her on January 4... In Chennai, on January 7, a 56-year-old employee of a private company, Muthu Palaniappan, killed his wife with a crowbar for fighting neighbours over TV noise. He told them later: 'I have solved the issue.'*

Then there's the event that may yet prove to be the game-changer for Indian society. On the night of December 16, 2012, a 23-year-old female medical student was assaulted in a moving van on the streets of Delhi. The victim and her boyfriend had accepted a lift with her three attackers, after failing to find an autorickshaw willing to drive them home. The woman was brutally gang-raped in front of her boyfriend and pummeled so forcibly with a metal bar that she died of her wounds, in a Singapore hospital, two weeks later. This, just one in a wave of grisly acts of sexual violence in the conservative Indian capital, broke the levee.

The event provoked the 'rape uprisings' of early 2013, as tens of thousands of protestors took to the streets, storming Delhi's late-colonial national monument, India Gate. These protests cast a bright light on the dark underside of modern India, as a watching global media heard relentless stories of everyday sexual abuse, and of an incompetent police and judicial system that does little to stop it.

It remains to be seen whether these events will spark a social revolution, or whether such changes will take generations to play out. In one positive move, however, in March 2013 the Indian Government passed a Rape Law that makes stalking, voyeurism and sexual harassment crimes (though it falls short of criminalising marital rape).

One thing is for sure: in India women's bodies – Indian women's bodies as well as those of Western women tourists – are a territory on which a societal war is being waged.

In her idea that Indian culture is the seedbed of such violence, D'mello is on to something. Dark depictions of sexual violence loom large in popular media. In a 2008 *Times of India* sex survey, rape was logged as the third most popular genre of porn. And until very recently, while kissing was forbidden in Bollywood, brutal rape scenes were a staple.

In his book *Intimate Relations: Exploring Indian Sexuality*, Indian psychiatrist Sudhir Kakar suggests that the confused Indian male is the real author of these leitmotifs, rather than vice versa. For the viewer to get his sexual gratification, and for Indian women to remain on their pedestal of virginity, contortions are necessary. Rape is the ready solution to this, the humiliation of women 'integral to the Indian male's fantasy of love'.

D'mello is not alone in her outrage. In one of the earliest direct action campaigns, in 2009, a non-violent protest group took on the leader of the Mangalore chapter of orthodox Hindu group Sri Ram Sene. This organisation, which had earlier attacked a group of girls for drinking at a Mangalore pub, had darkly threatened to 'take action' against unmarried couples caught together on Valentine's Day. Naming themselves the Pink Chaddi Campaign, a protest group retaliated by asking their supporters to send, on the same Valentine's Day, pairs of pink chaddis (underpants) in the post to Sri Ram Sene's headquarters – 250,000 pairs were dispatched.

Then came the Blank Noise Project, an anti-eve-teasing community public art initiative, with 50 per cent male membership, chapters across India, and tactics such as spray-painting the testimonies of rape victims in public spaces and staging exhibitions of the garments women were wearing when they were sexually molested. Despite Indian conservatives' demonisation of denim, most of these garments turned out to be traditional sarees and shalwar kameez. In the wake of the rape uprisings came Pepper the Pigs, asking patrons to donate, buy or request pepper sprays to arm Indian women, which garnered several hundred thousand rupees of donations in its first week.

In truth, says D'mello, the current situation with regard to sexual violence, in which Delhi tops a list of Indian cities when it comes to rapes per capita, is a simple case of old attitudes conflicting with the new: 'Delhi is a modern city, but it also has a large conservative Muslim population; it is also fast encroaching into surrounding farmland, where very traditional attitudes prevail.'

Even before the events of December 2012 propelled them onto the world stage, lurid reports of gang rapes, many in Delhi and the neighbouring areas, made headlines almost weekly. A notorious example is what became known as the 'Haryana raping spree', which claimed 20 young victims in a few weeks, including a 13-year-old disabled girl. One of the rape victims doused herself with kerosene and lit a match, and the *New York Times* reported that the father of another committed suicide after seeing an online video of his daughter's molestation.

What is equally horrifying to D'mello and the young Indians she represents is the reaction of some religious leaders to the country's soaring rates of reported and unreported rape. In the case of the Haryana rapes, a khap panchayat, one of the unelected boards of all-male tribal elders that hold significant sway in the villages, decided to get involved. The real problem, they decided, was child marriage, or the lack thereof: if the minimum marriageable age (currently 18 for females and 21 for males) was lowered to 15 or 16, they reasoned, unmarried boys wouldn't feel compelled to take out their sexual frustration on girls. When Indian politicians publicly endorsed this idea, four United Nations organisations wrote a joint letter to Indian Union Women and Child Development Minister Krishna Tirath, stating 'child marriage is not a solution to protecting girls from sexual crimes including rape'. The letter went on to remind the Indian Government that since 40 per cent of the world's child marriages already happen in India, the minimum marriageable age limits could not be to blame for the rise in sexual assaults.

The surreal responses to India's crisis didn't end there. The chief minister of another state, Bengal, threw in her hundred rupees' worth, suggesting that these gender-based crimes were a result of boys and girls commingling as never before, in an India that's 'an open market with open options'. Meanwhile Dharamvir Goyat, of the Congress party, opined that 90 per cent of the rape cases were consensual. A few weeks later, a khap panchayat in Haryana's Jind district blamed the growing incidence of rape on the consumption of chow mein, with thua khap panchayat leader Jitender Chhatar commenting: 'To my understanding, consumption of fast food contributes to such incidents. Chow mein leads to hormonal imbalance evoking an urge to indulge in such acts.'

The pinning of the blame for India's runaway rates of sexual violence on diet continued in November 2012 with the publication of *New Healthway*, a textbook aimed at 11- and 12-year-olds. It included the gem of wisdom that meat-eaters 'easily cheat, tell lies, forget promises and commit sex crimes'. The book, criticised by many Indian educators, also asserted that meat-eaters are dishonest, and Eskimos 'lazy' and 'sluggish' because of their meat consumption.

So D'mello sees herself as struggling not just against the prevalence of sexual violence in India, but also against rank stupidity. She sees Indian women as coming up against an uncomfortable truth: 'There are 830 women to every 1000 men in Haryana state. Haryanans abort their female foetuses then wonder why young men fed images of sexual violence with no access to legitimate sex go crazy. We're living in a country where there are too few vaginas to go around; where there are regressive attitudes towards women, and where's there's ready access to violent pornography. What other outcome could there be?'

Following the events of late 2012, Western commentators joined the rallying call for societal revolution in India: a revolution that would put the country on track towards the less troubled inter-gender relationships and sexual freedoms enjoyed in the West. But perhaps we in the West shouldn't be so quick to put ourselves forward as exemplars of smooth-running gender politics. After all, stalking, harassment and some forms of rape are on the rise in Western nations too.

A 2012 survey found that UK internet users with a female username are 25 times more likely to suffer a 'trolling' attack (online harassment) than a user with a male username. In many Western countries, rates of violent rape are increasing, especially those involving gangs and young perpetrators and victims.

In a typical incident in Richmond, California, in 2008, fellow students abducted a teenage girl as she left a school homecoming dance. As her father waited anxiously for her in the car park, she was violently raped by numerous assailants during an ordeal that lasted two and a half hours. One key component of the attack mirrors the December 2012 gang rape in Delhi: voyeurism, which appears to be a defining phenomenon of our age. Rather than calling for help or reporting the rape, young witnesses filmed and photographed it on their cell phones. This event was echoed in the prominent 2012 Steubenville High School rape case, in which a drugged 16-year-old Ohio schoolgirl was transported, undressed and sexually assaulted by her peers, several of whom documented the acts on social media.

Another disturbing development is increasing sexualisation. A 2009 American Psychological Association taskforce report on the sexualisation of young American girls found that over the previous 12 years, teenage girls had begun to see their key value as residing in their sexuality. 'When a child takes this belief system to heart,' read the APA report, 'they no longer feel as if they are OK if they're straight A students, or gifted musicians or athletes. Instead, if they're not sexy, they're not OK.'

For young Westerners and Indians alike, 'The new definition of love,' as US paediatrician Sharon Cooper puts it, 'is "send me a sexy picture of yourself".'

Should we be worried about this? If Steubenville and the Delhi uprisings have done anything they've galvanised a debate, in East and West alike, about the brute realities of our respective rape and internet porn cultures. Perhaps in fact, eve-teasing is the least of our problems.

5 | WHAT IT FEELS LIKE FOR A GIRL, Delhi

GIGs (Good Indian Girls) and BIGs (Bad Indian Girls)

Women are hardly ever known in their true light, though they may love men or become indifferent towards them, may give them delight or abandon them, or may extract from them all of the wealth that they possess.
—Kama Sutra, Burton translation, 1883

A week later, as the first of Delhi's winter fogs wraiths the black nighttime streets of upmarket Defence Colony, I'm waiting for three thoroughly modern Indian girls. Forty minutes late, Dimple, Akshaya and Simutra pull up outside my apartment with a screech. The commotion kicks a rich plume of brick dust into the body of fog, and scatters the neighbourhood's feral dogs, six of whom are lazing on my bungalow's veranda.

Akshaya – as she'd promised earlier, bellowing into her cell phone – is behind the wheel of her 'baby': a white lowered Suzuki with tinted windows and a growling exhaust pipe. The girls' boisterous arrival has awoken a street's worth of security guards, who rub their eyes and sit upright on their plastic garden seats, nursing the shotguns that, I strongly suspect, are leftovers from the Raj.

There are young Indian women such as D'mello, who are becoming activists and speaking out publicly against India's outrageous levels of sexual violence. And there are those like Dimple who, through their life choices, are making a visible stand against the contradictory expectations Indian society imposes on them. And then there are many millions of Indian women like Akshaya and Sumitra, undergoing their own private revolutions, juggling parental and societal expectations – being Good Indian Girls (GIGs) on the surface and Bad Indian Girls (BIGs) underneath.

The Introduction to a 2011 collection of short stories, *The Bad Indian Boy's Guide to the Good Indian Girl*, explains the contortions GIGs are expected to perform:

> *GIGdom is judged through a complex set of parameters on an unstable graph. You could be a gentle, refined, virginal, practical kind of GIG, but your halo is sure to be dulled if your mother runs away with the cook, or if you develop an unreasonable aversion to nice clothes and dinner parties... She is judged by the number of phones she carries; the boys whose company she keeps. She is not expected to be wholly innocent to the ways of love, but she must still bear the burden of knowledge – she must be ignorant about how to go about making a career as a porn star or pole dancer, for instance, but she must know how to read people's minds.*

Originally from Chandigarh, the moneyed capital of the Punjab, Akshaya and Sumitra are two of the first generation of young Indian women to try on a Western lifestyle for size. Controversially, they 'stay alone', sharing a three-bed duplex in Delhi with another 20-something girl. This feat, which required two years' lobbying of aunties as to the girls' unimpeachable honour, was hard-won. So Akshaya and Sumitra make the most of their triumph. They spend their weekends razzing around the city, talking about sex and boys, and nurturing cigarette-smoking, paan-chewing and whisky-drinking habits that would be enough to fell a Punjabi truck driver.

Akshaya's now driving us at speed, opinions and invectives spilling out either side of the cigarette that's clamped between her teeth.

'Chutiya... Move your stupid ass, man... Look at this driver, huh? Like I was saying before this little lund [penis] got in my way... As girls they make us pay 10,000 rupees [£188] more for our apartment rental. It's hush money; a bribe so the landlord won't poke his nose into our business. And then there's the cook: the cook busybodies in our fridge, judging our morals against how much we ate of our dinner, gossiping all around the neighbourhood.

'This is why we have to become smooth operators. We are crafty. We are forced to manage our double lives like secret agents. We know that the only way to win the game is to know how the game works.'

Dimple murmurs in agreement. She's been sitting morosely in the back of the car ever since I picked my way through paan leaves and cigarette wrappers and took my place next to Akshaya in the front passenger seat. She's gloomy, she'd told me, sotto voce over the headrest, after another row with her mother. After Shimla, when I'd taken up my apartment in Defence Colony, Dimple had returned to her son, ayah and maid at her apartment in Delhi's South Extension.

She'd returned, too, to growing pressure from her mother to get remarried to an ageing NRI (non-resident Indian) businessman based in the north London suburb of Harrow.

She'd bristled with anger about this a few days earlier. 'Not choosy these NRIs,' she tells me. 'Hah! Not choosy! That's because no one wants them now they can marry a man with prospects here in India... I know what happens to girls who go to London. They think it will be all cups of Earl Grey by the Thames, but they end up bored mad in some semi, in the rain, wearing sarees that went out of fashion a decade ago. One day, honest to god, I'll strangle mother with that Nalli dupatta of hers...'

Dimple may have escaped the slow death of her loveless marriage, but she hasn't shaken the shadow, always keeping pace behind the Indian woman, of the GIG.

With a crunch of gears we join the great Kingsway, or Rajpath, of Edwin Lutyens' New Delhi, that final flourish of British pomp architected in the waning days of the Raj. India Gate, the Arc de Triomphe–inspired memorial to the Indian dead in the First World War, looms to our right; to our left is the Dhjan Chand National Stadium, one of the key venues for the corruption embarrasment that was the 2010 Delhi Commonwealth Games.

At the intersection of Shahjahan Road, a boy hawker presses his upper body through my window, small arms heavy with glossy magazines wrapped in cellophane. At the top is a copy of this month's *Cosmopolitan India*, its coverline reading 'Jungle Sex! (Prepare for the wildest sex of your life!)'.

'So why does the *Hindustani Times* wonder why Indian women go mad?' Akshaya picks up her musings on GIGdom while simultaneously throwing the car sharply to the right, in the process almost clipping a two-stroke delivery van loaded with Kashmiri rugs. 'Why we get mental disorders and kill ourselves?'

'Akshaya. Bas! Slow down!' shouts Dimple.

'Madness and suicide are, the way I see it, very sane responses to the crazy situation for Indian women,' continues Akshaya, ignoring Dimple and speeding up. 'We have to be pretty, we have to be good, we have to make the tea and smile at auntie. We have to have no lives and no sex; we have to look curvy and thin and white. We have to hold up the whole of Indian society on these thin, white ladylike shoulders. Chut ka maindak!'

Chut ka maindak, or 'frog in a vagina', is a regular in Akshaya's colourful repertoire of Hindi expletives. It soon becomes a firm favourite of mine among her lively argot.

Statistics corroborate the grim social reality she describes. A Nielsen study in 2011 (reported in *TIME* magazine), found India to be the most stressful country on earth for women, with 87 per cent of Indian female respondents reporting 'feeling stressed most of the time', to 74 per cent of women in second most stressed place Mexico. In a 2012 poll of humanitarian and gender specialists, a study that inspired outrage in the Indian press, India was labelled the worst place in the world to be a woman, taking into account factors such as infanticide, child marriage, the persistence of the dowry tradition (despite its illegality) and slavery.

In another appalling statistic, in March 2013 the *British Medical Journal* reported that suicide had become the primary cause of death in Indian women aged from 18 to 49, overtaking the former principal cause, death during childbirth, by several tens of thousands a year.

Akshaya, Dimple and I dust off a stone picnic bench and sit down to eat. We're at Dilli Haat, an open-air food-hall-cum-craft-bazaar run by the Delhi Tourism and Transport Development Corporation. This popular bazaar, which opened in 1994 and now has a sister market in North Delhi, attracts criticism from the chattering classes for the way its clothing and jewellery stalls make a spectacle of tribespeople, dressed up in traditional regional costumes and paid a pittance for the entertainment of big-city Delhiites.

Less contentious, Dilli Haat's regional food stalls are favoured by young Delhiites. They're a favourite of mine too, offering edible snapshots of the cuisines India has gifted the world: from the light, tamarind-tempered flavours of the south to the heavy, tandoor-oven-cooked dishes popularised by the Mughals. We've chosen Maharastra, and order from a youth at the counter.

'The problem,' Akshaya continues as we wait for our food, 'is all this goddess rubbish. So the bhartiya naari [ideal Indian woman] is the goddess Lakshmi as a bride crossing her husband's threshold, bringing wealth and luck. She is Saraswati giving the wisdom to her children. She is a Devi [divine] as her husband's strength. And the goddess is not just in the temple. She's in Bollywood, too: these perfect white goddesses, up there on their pedestals.'

The food arrives and Akshaya quickly gets stuck in, loading bhel puri – the puffed rice, potato and chutney snack synonymous with Bombay – into her mouth like a stevedore filling a ship's hold.

'Either on her pedestal or down in the gutter,' chips in Dimple with a dark laugh, 'and there's no climbing back up. I think they burnt the ladder.'

'And god help her if she becomes a mortal,' Akshaya says, wiping her mouth.

'Did you see what happened to Aishwarya last week?' Dimple asks.

Aishwarya Rai, model and actress, humanitarian face of L'Oréal and former Miss India and Miss World, had a few months earlier given birth to her first child by her Bollywood actor husband. With Rai still plump a couple of months after the birth, the Indian gossip press was quick to sharpen its claws: 'From fit babe to fat auntie' gloated one news daily.

'Hah! At least they didn't attack her for having a girl,' says Sumitra, as she pours a round of Thums Ups for the table. With double the sweetness of Coca-Cola, this sickly beverage is a favourite of young Indians, despite the feverish efforts of Western brands such as Mountain Dew to gain purchase in the booming Indian market. I take a sip and feel my molars flinch.

'You know, I went to a wedding the other week and met a doctor who's set up a hospital at Hyderabad to change girl babies into boy babies,' Akshaya continues. '"Regendering services" he called it. Chut ka maindak! I thought it was bad enough all the infanticides, all the girl babies found in the trashcans.'

I wonder what the girls might make of the depictions of the ideal Indian woman in the Kama Sutra, so I retrieve my dog-eared copy and read out a passage from the Introduction, in which Burton hymns the Hindu ideal of perfect feminine excellence, the Lotus woman:

> *Her face is pleasing as the full moon; her body, well clothed with flesh, is soft as the Shiras or mustard flower; her skin is fine, tender and fair as the yellow lotus, never dark-coloured.... She has three folds or wrinkles across her middle – about the umbilical region. Her yoni resembles the opening lotus bud, and her love seed (Kama salila) is perfumed like the lily that has newly burst... She eats little, sleeps lightly... she is clever and courteous.*

Akshaya snorts at this. 'I recognise her. She's a mannequin, not a woman.'

She's right; I recognise the lotus woman too. Here is the Indian woman packaged as fantasy fodder for the male consumer; a consumer common to many times and continents, from Victorian Britons to modern-day Indians.

Happily, in Book Six of the Kama Sutra things get a bit more interesting. We meet the Gupta Empire's professional courtesans: ambitious businesswomen, picky lovers and pursuers of sexual pleasure.

Here the courtesan is advised to retain her self-respect, playing men for the weaknesses of their nature and – for all the vagaries of passion – keeping her shrewd eye trained on financial gain: 'A courtesan should not sacrifice money to love, because money is the chief thing to be attended to.'

'Huh. I wish that wasn't true today,' says Dimple when I read out this passage. 'But it is. Many Indian girls can't afford love. Because what price does it come at? Being disowned by your family for not having the arranged marriage with the engineer? Having no future?'

Rather than hectoring advice directed at an underclass, I've often felt that the tone of Book Six reads more like *The Rules*, Ellie Fein and Sherrie Schneider's hugely successful 1995 self-help book. Subtitled 'Time-Tested Secrets for Capturing the Heart of Mr. Right', *The Rules* was a publishing sensation in the West, offering, among its decrees for playing hard-to-get, such tips as 'Don't Accept a Saturday Night Date', 'Don't Call Him and Rarely Return His Calls' and the more enigmatic 'Be a Creature Unlike Any Other'.

Compare that to the Kama Sutra's methodologies for courtesans to bag their prize: 'Even though she is invited by a man to join him, she should not at once consent to a union, because men are apt to despise things which are easily acquired.' Both advisories play up to male predilections for the chase and vaunt the majesties of the female mystique, however imagined. As Vatsyayana puts it at his book's close, rather longingly:

> *The extent of the love of women is not known, even to those who are the objects of their affection, on account of its subtlety, and on account of the avarice and natural intelligence of womankind.*

Today's young Indian women should have the luck of Vatsyayana's courtesans. Compiled by a young Indian author, *The Bad Boy's Guide to the Good Indian Girl* poignantly bemoans the situation of the modern Indian woman. Rather than projecting a dangerous mystique, theirs is to aim for the goddess ideal of the demure bhartiya naari:

> *There are hundreds of communities on the subcontinent, and not all of them place the same value on innocence – sexual or social. But they lie on the fringes of our cultural consciousness. When people talk about the 'bhartiya naari', the image that pops into our heads is of a saree-clad woman with long hair, someone demure and skilled at housework. We do not think of the tobacco-chewing field labourer with muscles on her arms and a song on her lips. Both are equally Indian, of course.*

It's getting very late as we pile back into the Suzuki for what Akshaya, with a mysteriousness befitting a Kama Sutra courtesan, has advertised as 'some wildlife spotting'. I'd turned the topic of conversation to sex. How, in a society that expects them to project virginity, do these Good Indian Girls have fun, as they all profess to do?

'That's the thing with Good Indian Girls,' Akshaya says, as she reverses out at 50 m.p.h. onto a main road. 'Good Indian Girls aren't good. We only have to *appear* to be good to our elders, our family. As far as they want to know we're working hard, thinking about finding a suitable husband. And we act that way: we keep everything sweet; we smile and serve the chai to our grandpa. We know we have to preserve the nation by being virgins and having no fun. So we have our other lives, with our friends and our lovers.'

In a handful of years, the average age of first sexual experience for Indian girls has dropped from 22 to 19 years. *India Today*'s 2008 sex survey painted a picture of the new Indian female. In 2003, 57 per cent of Indian women respondents to the survey said premarital sex was wrong and 78 per cent said they were against extramarital sex; as of 2012 these statistics have declined to 46 per cent and 66 per cent respectively. Surveys also hint at a rise in female assertiveness in relationships. In 2003, 61 per cent of women said they would talk and sort it out if their partner was unfaithful to them, compared with just 37 per cent six years later.

Then there's the phenomenon that must affect young Indian women, and is indeed held by many as a key contributory factor to Delhi's rape crisis: the pornification of the Indian media. In a 2012 issue cover-lined 'Desi Porn Boom', desi being the slang term for the people or products of the subcontinent, *India Today* again laid out the facts. According to Google Trends, the number of IP addresses undertaking searches for porn in India doubled between 2010 and 2012; in 2011, seven Indian cities were among the world's top ten in terms of the frequency of searches for porn. In the same year, a survey of independent schools in Delhi revealed that 47 per cent of students discuss porn every day. No comparison figure is available for the West.

Emblematic of the nation's pornography preoccupation are three Karnataka ministers who, in early 2012, were photographed viewing porn clips in state assembly. The images made it onto Indian newspaper front pages, yet the politicians were unapologetic about being rumbled. A Delhi friend explained the immunity powerful Indians enjoy when it comes to moral and familial affairs as follows: 'In Anglo-Saxon countries, your neighbours can do anything, but your politicians, such as Bill Clinton, can't get away with a thing. In India, it's the other way round. Your neighbours have to be on their best behaviour, and it's the politicians who get up to the hanky-panky.'

The same month as the Indian porngate scandal, the *Times of India* colourfully reported the case of a woman driven to viricide by her husband's 'porn addiction': 'Anita, 30, a homemaker in Betul, Madhya Pradesh, who had never dared refuse her husband Ramcharan's increasing demands for "unnatural" sex, would just snap. When he started to display indecent video clippings on his mobile, she picked up a stone and smashed his head in.'

But it's not just frustrated young men and bored civil servants who are consuming all of this porn. While one in five Indian women in the 2008 *India Today* survey claimed to approve of pornography, the proportion of those actually watching it is higher, with nearly one in four saying they have viewed it. The incidence of porn watching among women is particularly high in the southern city of Chennai and in Delhi. One in ten porn-watching Indian women, according to the report, said that they would be open, if asked, to participating in a porn video.

So how does it feel, I ask Akshaya and Sumitra, to operate in an ostensibly sexually conservative country that's effectively basting itself in hardcore pornography?

'Some things are good,' says Akshaya. 'You can buy sex toys in Delhi now. They're still illegal, but you go to this guy at an electronics shop in Karol Bagh, say a code word, and he gets it for you from the upstairs shop. In other ways it's not so good. Men expect all these moves they see in these porn clips on their handphones, but then think badly of their girlfriend if she does them. In this way, we cannot win.'

At last we've reached our destination. Akshaya orders us out of the car with 'Go! Go! Go!' – a shouty injunction employed by many Indian women that I've long ago learned not to be offended by.

'It's a good hour for wildlife spotting,' she says with relish, as we push through an entrance choked with autos plying for trade into the bosky calm of Lodi Gardens.

Ninety acres of emerald lawns dotted with neem and palm trees – home in the winter months to migratory pied cuckoos and blue-throats sheltering from the European chill and in summer to wagtails, mynahs and sulphur-bellied white-throats – Lodi Gardens is a popular recreation spot for Delhiites. In that way that Indians have of living around and on top of their history rather than roping it off as we do in the West, the gardens are arranged around the tombs – onion-domed, crumbling and colonnaded – of the Lodis: Sunni Muslims and the last of the Delhi Sultanates.

Gardens have long been considered an appropriate place of courtship for Indian couples. The Kama Sutra advises the practice of going to gardens or picnics as an aspect of good citizenry:

> *In the forenoon, men, having dressed themselves, should go to gardens on horseback, accompanied by public women and followed by servants. And having done there all the duties of the day, and passed the time in various agreeable diversions, such as the fighting of quails, cock and rams, and other spectacles, they should return home in the afternoon in the same manner, bringing with them bunches of flowers.*

The diversions induged in today in Indian parks are not so innocent.

Akshaya has brought us to see what for many young Indians passes as a date. In the past few years, outdoor urban sex nests have blossomed in India, prompting anxious column inches in the national press. These became a torrent in early 2011, when the mangrove jungle abutting Bombay's

Girgaum Chaupati beach was found to be home to state-of-the-art love nests. Managed by a young city entrepreneur, these were rented out for 100 rupees an hour and fitted with shale floors and mosquito coils.

We're not at the beach, though, but walking into the depths of the gardens at Lodi, where weeping willows graze the grass and the thick bush growth provides nooks shielded from the immediate sight of the pathways. As my eyes adjust to the nighttime gloom, I notice a young couple. The man, perhaps 20 years old, wears a Metallica T-shirt; his female companion sits on his lap, her saree rucked up and her hair in an advanced state of disarray. The woman turns round, spots us, and then resumes her furtive fumbling.

'She's checking we're not police,' says Akshaya in a thick whisper that must be audible to our happy couple. 'The police usually blackmail the youngsters for bribes, saying they'll tell their parents, or even beat them with the lathi [the thin Indian truncheon].'

Ah, I think to myself, so much for the Good Indian Girl.

Keen to know more about how and why young Indians are suddenly seeking space to be together, flouting societal pressure and enjoying furtive sexual escapades, I meet Nandini Bhalla at the office block where she edits *Cosmopolitan India*, a magazine famous for its sexual explicitness in the West but which, in its Indian incarnation, walks the tightrope of innocence and sexual exploration along with its confused readers.

Up on the block's rooftop, between tendrils of cigarette smoke, Bhalla tells me, 'It's all changed in the past five or ten years. Indian women are leaving their arranged marriages. They're seeking financial independence. They've changed.

But they've only changed, say, 50 per cent. We have to give really basic sex advice: nothing to scare the woman off. It has to be quite vanilla, and refer to her husband, of course. It is aaallll about sex with the husband.'

Lighting her second cigarette from the lipsticky stub of her first, Bhalla sounds exasperated. 'Our Hindu gods are always fucking, for chrissake. But Indian conservatives expect us all to be virgins. But they're living in a fantasy. Young Indian women are doing it; or want to do it. Not in S&M dungeons in New York like Samantha Jones in *Sex and the City*, not with fluffy handcuffs, usually in snatched moments in parked cars. But they are doing it.'

6 | WHAT IT FEELS LIKE FOR A BOY, Delhi

In search of the new Indian male – meeting the gigolos

A man's natural talent is his roughness and ferocity,
A woman's is her lack of power
And her suffering, self-denial and weakness.
Their passion and a particular technique
May sometimes lead them to exchange roles;
But not for very long. In the end.
The natural roles are re-established.

—Kama Sutra, Book Two,
Doniger/Kakar translation, 2002

The Diwali cracker smog is finally clearing and the Delhi air losing its old-clothes autumnal smell when, one morning a couple of weeks later, Dimple and I take an auto to Gulmohar Park Journalists' Colony, a green and affluent neighbourhood in South Delhi. We have an appointment with Rahul Roy, a documentary filmmaker, writer and journalist on the theme of masculine identity.

'For Indian men, gender is a straitjacket,' he says, in a tiny office that's stacked floor to ceiling with books and DVDs.

Dimple and I drink milky chai from small white cups balanced on our knees, for want of desk space.

'Men and women have very fixed identities in India, but at the same time the realities of life are changing,' Roy continues. 'For lower-caste men and women who come into the city, women's incomes are more reliable. They'll have a full-time job, as an ayah maybe, and their husband will work shift-work, which is intermittent. The man is no longer the breadwinner and this skews the power balance.

'What you end up with is what we have now: a huge power shift. This power shift will ultimately give us better relationships, but it also has its victims. Rapes are on the increase in the news, as are honour killings.'

He's right that the outlook isn't totally gloomy for all Indian women: some have made great strides in recent decades. Middle-class women's school achievements outstrip those of men, and women have moved forcefully into many industries, although their workforce participation is much lower than that of men, or women, in the West (29 per cent in 2008–12 against 56 per cent in the UK and 58 per cent in the US). Middle-class women in India have broken the glass ceiling in traditionally male sectors such as banking and finance (with greater success at the CEO level, in fact, than in Western countries) and have also become increasingly visible in the upper echelons of Indian politics.

However, these – the most fortunate of women in India rising – are coming into conflict with a vast and growing cohort of low-skilled, unattached and unemployed young men. Thanks to the past few decades' heady rates of female infanticide (as the use of ultrasound gendering has boomed), these men have no hope of attaining wives and have come to view women's success as the cause of their own romantic and economic failure.

'Women are breaking through and advancing toward greater attainment,' Dr K. Srinath Reddy, president of the Public Health Foundation of India, told the *International Herald Tribune*. 'One of the natural manifestations of that tension is increased violence against women.'

All of this is to be expected, says Roy, from a generation of young males who've been spoon-fed a very narrow definition of what might define their self-worth. Indian boy children are often indulged by their parents in behaviours seen as powerful and manly, such as rumbustious squabbling and war-play. They are also breastfed for longer, given more of the family food rations and suffer substantially reduced mortality rates compared to Indian girl children; United Nations data from 2012 found that an Indian girl child is 75 per cent more likely to die before her fifth birthday than an Indian boy.

'There's a great emphasis in India on male "performance",' continues Roy, 'with work; with women. It's a very narrow set of norms and, as a result, the men who don't match up feel a sense of fragility and failure. This, in turn, makes them lash out.'

He is not merely pontificating: he actually takes on these tight social definitions, in his movie making and in the occasional workshops he runs on Indian masculinity and its meanings. He's part of an explosion of initiatives on similar themes in India, including NGO-run projects among migrant workers in Bombay, to help them adjust to that city's relatively liberated women, and Must Bol/Let's Talk, a 'male sensitisation project' targeting Delhi youth around issues of sexual violence and gender.

Of course, the West hasn't been immune to such problems, although rates of domestic violence and male uxoricide peaked in the West between the 1880s and 1930s. Domestic violence was especially pronounced in frontier territories and colonies, communities in which – and here there are echoes in modern India – manliness was prized and women were scarce.

But what defines manliness? According to historian Ronald Hyam, by the turn of the twentieth century the nineteenth-century notions of what made the ideal Victorian male were transformed, in 'a shift from serious earnestness to robust virility, from integrity to hardness'. There was a focus on Spartan habits and discipline, the cultivation of all that was masculine and the expulsion of all that was 'effeminate, unEnglish and excessively intellectual'. Manliness moved from 'chapel to changing room [to become] a pervasive middle-class code'.

Beards and competitive sports – those two enduring exports to the colonies – became ciphers for this manliness. Edward Lyttelton, headmaster of Eton in the 1880s, memorably complained that the school's new smooth pitches made cricket 'worthless' as 'they removed pain from the game'.

This emphasis was to evolve, in later decades, into the cult of the emphatically physical, or machismo. This was to give us the Nazi semiotics of the virile Aryan male in the 1930s and the US ideal of the broad-chested family man in the 1950s. Later, it would feed into advertising phenomena that lionised manliness, often with a nostalgic tenor, such as the Marlboro and Camel men.

In the West, of course, the 1990s gave us the New Male: a man as comfortable with hands-on fathering as he is with the pharmacy's moisturiser counter. But the New Indian Male – or the absence thereof – is a hot topic in modern India. Mukul Kesavan, author of *The Ugliness of the Indian Male and Other Propositions*, argues that Indian men have no incentive to become New Indian Males. After all, they can choose an arranged marriage with a homely girl rather than adapt themselves to appeal to the New Indian Girl.

'Indian men are ugly on account of the three Hs: hygiene, hair and horrible habits,' she says. 'Despite the way they look, they're always paired off with good-looking women.'

In a 2009 op-ed entitled 'Why Indian Men Are Still Boys', Indian journalist Nisha Susan, one of the brains behind the Pink Chaddi protest, defined the all too common phenomenon of the Old Indian Male succinctly. You can almost hear her sigh:

> *The man who finds it difficult to deal with his girlfriend's higher income; who assumes all young women are interns or secretaries or have slept their way up the professional ladder; who assumes his teenage sister-in-law does not mind his copping a feel as long as she stays under his roof; who discusses the difference between analytic and synthetic philosophy with his students while forgetting to introduce the wife who brings in tray after tray of coffee.*

A few days later, in a Café Coffee Day coffee shop in a district full of jeans-wearing teenagers, we meet 22-year-old Pallab and 34-year-old Lakhan, along with their agent Goutam. Pallab and Lakhan reveal another side of the male–female power coin, selling an idealised male identity back to moneyed female customers. They are male gigolos and strippers, and are among a burgeoning number of young Indian males who work as full-time or 'flying' (part-time) sex workers.

Pallab's reasons for going into casual prostitution are familiar: he needed to support his family back in Madhya Pradesh, but wanted to continue his studies during daylight hours. He began in the business, he tells me, by cruising for trade in the luxuriant botanical gardens of his home city

Kolkata (formerly Calcutta). He was 18 and was struck by how easy it all was.

'I was surprised,' he tells me. 'You could see sexual desire in these women's eyes. They would approach me on a bench and ask for directions, and I'd maybe ask for a light. Then, moments later, the deal would be struck and I'd follow the woman to her car.'

Pallab eventually gave up his studies, moved to Delhi and became a stripper and gigolo full time.

There are few phenomena as indicative of the shift in socially acceptable behaviour underway in India as gigolo parties. Partly driven by the desires of liberal, returnee NRIs, their risqué mood was captured in the Bollywood movie *Oops!* This 2003 film follows aspiring dancers Jagan and Akash as they are pulled into an underworld of dancing strip for high-society women. It portrayed a scene in its ascendance, a couple of brief years when Delhi nightclubs were offering promotional nights featuring women-only entry and male strippers.

This all changed in 2005 when an Indian television channel ran a hidden-camera exposé on one of the clubs, and a similar 'ladies night' made newspaper headlines in the southern city of Chennai. The resultant hue and cry pushed the male strip scene underground, into private homes and out-of-town parties.

But it didn't suppress the popularity of the trend. Today, it's not just high-society women who are enjoying the titillation of young, stripteasing males; middle-class women are getting in on the act too. Major cities have unofficial gigolo pick-up points, and 'male model' agencies, targeting strip parties, are booming. In a litmus test of these appetites, in a 2012 Indian sex habits survey conducted by *India Today* magazine, 49 per cent of women respondents reported that they'd like to attend a male stripper show.

And it's a competitive business. Now in his early 30s, Lakhan tells me of his concerns about younger boys snatching his livelihood: 'I've been doing this for seven years, and now the women like them skinny and younger and younger. Many boys I do these party jobs with are 16, 17.'

Goutam, in a low whisper, chips in to agree. 'Yes, these days the women like the boys young. Wheatish [pale-skinned] boys, skinny, but tall like in the Punjab.'

I ask Lakhan and Pallab about the challenges of rising to the job.

'I'm OK, but many of the older men have to take Viagra,' Lakhan replies. 'We get it off the internet, but sometimes it's really amphetamine or talcum and doesn't work. And you can't risk having many bad nights. There's a lot, you know, about reputation in this career.'

I ask him whether he used protection. He nods and pulls out a packet of KamaSutra LongLast. India's second biggest condom brand, KamaSutras were an edgy product when they launched in 1991, featuring one of the first Indian ad campaigns to emphasise sensuality rather than safety, and starring two top models of the time, Pooja Bedi and Mark Robinson, naked, oiled and bound around each other with a live cobra.

'So what is your plan B?' Dimple asks Lakhan, with concern in her voice. 'What will you do when you're too old for this game?'

'I don't know,' he says, suddenly looking his full 34 years, the worry registering on his face. 'I think I'll have to run my own boys. There's no work for me back in my village. There's mining, but it's dirty and dangerous, run by mafia bosses who bring in their own cheap men from the East. I have my sister's family to support. Her husband died down the mine. So what do I do, get a 10,000 rupee a month job as a waiter? Watch them starve?'

Nevertheless, he's disillusioned. If it wasn't for the money he'd get out of the flesh game, he tells us. 'Women have become very demanding. Sometimes they shock me with their demands. Sometimes they book me for a weekend, then don't pay me and threaten to call the police and say I raped them. Sometimes they burn my body with cigarettes.'

Goutam, the men's agent, looks momentarily ill at ease, but goes on to confide that business is good. 'Now I run my operations out of Bombay and Delhi the same. My clients are real hi-fi women. They have busy husbands. They can't get enough of my boys.'

Operating from a laptop on the road and working under a pseudonym, he has over 200 men on his books, most of whom he picks up via personal ads, or by targeting wannabe actors and models through social networking sites such as Facebook. Goutam's boys cost from around 5000 rupees for a night up to 250,000 rupees for a 'name' gigolo, famous South Asian actors and models whose identities he won't disclose.

Looking at these three men, with their multiple cell phones, tight T-shirts stretched over gym-buffed torsos and crisply gelled hair, I wonder about the implications of India's booming market for male bodies for sale.

The rise of the Indian gigolo certainly speaks of a new breed of Indian alpha women and a shift in the traditional power balance, at least in some sections of society. These women – a privileged group of moneyed wives often nicknamed the 'aunties' – have the economic freedom to seek something apart from a loveless relationship. They are profiting, ostensibly, from the new Indian dream, with their lattice of servants and home help, their free hours and their mod cons.

But in many ways, and in spite of their modernity, these women are consuming the old status symbols: servants, sexy young boys, people of the lower castes who are to be had as readily as a new cell phone. All in all, it doesn't feel much like progress.

*

Back in Gulmohar Park, Dimple had asked Roy if he was positive about the future of the modern Indian male. She looked wide-awake and hopeful, as if her future happiness might ride on his answer. Our chai cups had been cleared away by a male servant, who gingerly fished them out from among the literary ephemera that blanketed the desk. Roy seemed small and thoughtful amid his towering landscape of papers and books.

'The emotional journeys that are being made by Indian men and women are very different,' he said. 'And make no mistake. What you're seeing is two revolutions: a social revolution and a sexual revolution. Change will come – it is coming.'

7 | WHAT IT FEELS LIKE FOR A HIJRA, Gujarat

At a retirement home for eunuchs and gay men

There are two sorts of persons of the third nature, in the form of a woman and in the form of a man. The one in the form of a woman imitates a woman's dress, chatter, grace, emotions, delicacy, timidity, innocence, frailty and bashfulness... The one in the form of a man, however, conceals her desire when she wants a man.

—Kama Sutra, Book Two, On Sexual Union,
Doniger/Kakar translation, 2002

I've left Delhi and am heading to Rajpipla, a small town in the conservative state of Gujarat. Today's Rajpipla is sleepy by the standards of this nation of 1.2 billion people, its 50,000 inhabitants scratching a living via agriculture, middle-of-the-road private education and small-scale garment production.

But for many hundreds of years, things were very different. Until 1948, Rajpipla was the seat of the prosperous princely state of the Gohil Rajputs, commanding an area that spanned 1500 square miles, bounded by the Narmada and Tapti rivers, and taking in forests and fertile agricultural plains as well as the agate-rich Saptura mountains.

The Gohil Rajput's 600-year reign ended in the same way as many of the old Maharajas'. Following Indian Independence in 1947, the Kingdom of Rajpipla was one of the first to accede, in 1948, to the newly created Indian state. The last Maharaja, the anglophile Vijaysinhji, quietly retreated to Old Windsor, his estate in Berkshire, where he died three years later. For many such men the story would have ended in a similarly obscure fashion, but for the efforts of canny descendants to work their remaining assets – personal and property – in the emergent palace-hospitality trade.

The Gohil Rajputs did manage to adapt one of their properties, the 1910 Rajpant palace complex, into a luxury hotel. Now painted flamingo pink, with white Corinthian columns, the hotel is popular for local weddings and conferences attended by quiet Gujarati businessmen. This is where Dimple and I have arrived, dusty after the onward journey from the hub railway line at Miyagam Karjan, for an audience with the Gohil Rajput, who's responsible for keeping not only Rajpipla but the old Indian royals on the world map: Manvendra Singh Gohil, Vijaysinhji's grandson, India's first openly gay prince and the champion of third genders, the social group within which hijras, or eunuchs, are the most famous tier.

I'd heard Manvendra Singh Gohil's name a number of times over the years, during my visits to India and back in the West. I'd learned that in 2002, after a nervous breakdown, Singh Gohil had come out to the Indian public; and that the subsequent scandal had caused him to be excommunicated from the Gohil Rajput clan. I'd heard news reports about his social activism and had seen his campy 2007 outing on the Oprah Winfrey special 'Gay around the World', the first of two appearances on the show of a woman who's become one of Singh Gohil's several Western patrons.

I'd also seen him in glossy magazine spreads, got up in royal silks and turbans, often being interviewed about his earliest homosexual experiences, which were fumbled and conducted with his personal servant boy when Gohil was aged 12. Recently, I'd noticed that stories about Singh Gohil had focused on his ambition to adopt an heir, a decision Western reports had vaunted as 'the first gay adoption in India' ... 'Gay man in India adopts child! A first!'

I've thought since how these reports say much about our narrow interpretation, in the West, of homosexuality and Indian society. Because it's not a first at all, as far as Singh Gohil and his new 'gay son-in-law', young University of Bristol–educated engineer Deepak, are concerned.

'In many of India's old gender-variant communities, effeminate men would become mothers,' says Singh Gohil, as we sit with views out to the seven acres of elevated palace grounds, the river at their feet a gleaming tributary of the Narmada that once transported the agate that made much of his forebears' wealth. At the door, a waiter looks on, chewing a toothpick with the nonchalance of a movie cowboy.

'There is an ancient ceremony of third genders. I plan to do it with Deepak,' Singh Gohil explains. 'I will squeeze milk into his mouth to signify that "this is my milk; you are my child", and he will become my son. Many third-gender communities have had traditions like this for centuries: the Launda tradition in Bihar [the neighbouring Indian state to Uttar Pradesh, where Varanasi is located], for example, in which an older third-gender man adopts a younger son-cum-servant as his charge. Like those young twinkly twank boys in the US...

'The Britishers broke the third genders,' he continues. 'They called third genders "a breach of public decency" and placed them under the 1871 Criminal Tribes Act. This meant that, right up to Indian Independence, hijras were under constant surveillance and could be searched and arrested without warrant...

'So, it was a moral crusade. But it was also about power. After the Sepoy Mutiny the Britishers looked at who was influential. And, at the time, the third genders held the power. They had money, and their own tax structures and communities, or guranas, like royal courts. Some of the guranas had a heritage that could be traced back for 800, 1000 years. They had their own languages and idiolects. And there were different groups: the Koti, the Alis and the Hijras, with their own rich cultures and traditions.

'It's always been the case that the castrated hijra is most respected,' asserts Gohil. 'Today there are three kinds of third genders: mahbet hijras, or mother's bed hijras, who were born with confused genitals and were often given to the hijra community as children, or gravitated towards it themselves as older children or teenagers; nirwath hijras, who have male genitals but consider themselves female, they undergo the transition to become hijras, with some being castrated, some not; and naviyug or "new era" hijras, these are like the Bangkok ladyboys, they have breast implants and hormones, sometimes penises, sometimes not.'

It's a testament to the deep roots of their tradition that hijra communities survived the crackdowns of the Raj and the continuing ignominies ever since. The latter are very real. Today, most hijras live at the margins of society, eking out a living as sex workers; performing as musicians at ceremonies (typically on the birth of male babies); begging, or soliciting money with menaces. The April hijra festival in Koovagam, Tamil Nadu, when hundreds of thousands of third-gender women meet to reenact the story of the god Krishna disguising himself as a woman to marry Aravaan, a great warrior who was about to be sacrificed, has in recent years deteriorated into a prostitution fair and an opportunity for gangs of young Indian men to attack and sexually harass the hijras.

Violence against hijras, especially at the hands of the police, is widespread and brutal. However, an unhappy relationship with authorities is by no means universal. In 2006, for example, the city of Patna in the northern state of Bihar announced that hijras, known for their effective scare tactics, would thenceforth accompany its city revenue officials to collect unpaid taxes, receiving a 4 per cent commission on collected debts. And in October 2012, a case was put before the Indian Supreme Court to give hijras official status as a third gender and prevent them from being a 'legal non-entity', denied access to education, healthcare and public spaces.

As a social campaigner, Singh Gohil sees all of these sexually 'other' characters – gay men in the new definition, sexual outsiders in the old – as his kin. In 2009, he and a group of campaigners that included Indian novelist Vikram Seth and Nobel laureate economist Amartya Sen vigorously campaigned for an amendment to section 377 of the 1860 Indian penal code, which had criminalised gay sex – as it had any sexual activity that was determined 'against the natural order' (non-vaginal or inter-gender). They scored a triumph, and a historic judgment, when the High Court of Delhi gave legal effect to the decriminalisation of same-sex sexual behaviour among consenting adults. The amendment effectively undid the 150-year-old legislation against homosexual acts instituted by the British.

However, as Singh Gohil is keen to point out, the battle is not yet won. Immediately a flurry of appeals was filed against the legalisation. Campaigns were fronted by prominent Indian personalities, including Hindu holy man Swami

Ramdev, a pop spiritual leader known for his mass yoga camps, television shows and claims to cure cancer via the medium of breathing exercises. Ramdev had said, in advance of the judgment, 'This verdict of the court will encourage criminality and sick mentality. It is against our Vedic system! This is breaking the family system in India. Homosexuality is not natural and can be treated. If the government brings this law, I will take this matter to the streets of Delhi in protest.' And he did. Ramdev also added – in an echo of the Christian 'gay conversion' camps that proliferate in the American Midwest – that he could cure homosexuals of their 'illness' within six months using 'yoga, pranayam and other meditation techniques'.

It was an offer that Singh Gohil publicly accepted. 'I said I'd give him six months with my gay family. I said, "You try to convert me, and if you can't you need to withdraw your petition from the High Court." So we invited Ramdev to Rajpipla, and we didn't hear a thing. It was all bluster.'

I wonder if Singh Gohil shares the key idea of 'Indian sex guru' Bhagwan Shree Rajneesh, or Osho, whom we'll meet later, that sexual repression within religion inevitably leads to an unhealthy obsession with sex? As an illustration, I tell him, Deepak and a wide-eyed Dimple something I'd heard from an Iranian artist based in London who had been designated a 'religious pervert' by the Tehrani authorities for the crime of having Western women, with exposed décolletages, as Facebook friends. He had told me about the peculiar work of a select cadre of Shiite ayatollahs based in the Iranian capital who spend their days ruminating on rhetorical sexual quandaries, for example: 'There's an earthquake in my house and my aunt falls through the ceiling onto my erect penis. Is this halal, or is it haram?'

Singh Gohil smiles and considers this, as he signals our departure with a flick of the regal wrist to a nearby waiter.

We drain our milky morning coffees and head out through the hotel's marble-floored reception. On the way we pass through a gloomy drawing room that's littered with heavy Victorian tables, royal portraits and black metal European-style statutory; and then a banqueting hall, in which a 24-seat dining table is overlooked by photographs of Maharajah Vijaysinhji's exploits at the races and polo. As we stand at the crested portico of his fantasy palace, awaiting a driver, Singh Gohil draws breath and responds.

'Many religious men are, by their nature, hypocrites. Marriage pressures are so strong in India that if you don't want to marry, the only way out is to renounce the world. So, many gay men become religious ascetics to conceal their sexual preferences... And this is not just in India. I know this because many religious men have made a pass at me: Western Catholic priests and archbishops I have met and won't name.

'So the bigger problem, as I see it, comes from the pressure in India to marry: 85 per cent of MSMs [men who have sex with men] will be married.'

Dimple interjects, 'That's not just in rural India either, you know. I have a good girlfriend who had an arranged marriage to a gay man when she was aged 20. She's 32 now and her life is in pieces. Her husband rapes her from his hatred: for himself and his situation.'

'Yes,' says Singh Gohil, 'it ruined my wife's life too, which I deeply regret. I married at 26, to a girl from a good family in Madhya Pradesh. I thought after marriage that I would be all right because I never knew – and nobody told me – that I was gay, and [that] this was OK. So the marriage never got consummated, and I quickly realised I had done something very wrong. We divorced when I confided to my wife that I was gay. But it was only when I was hospitalised aged 37 with a nervous breakdown that my family found out.

'Yet I was lucky, in a way,' he continues. 'The real tragedies can come when a man marries and continues to have MSM sex, discreetly. If he manages to have sex with his wife too, she will never imagine he's gay, so it's the perfect alibi. The problem, of course, comes when he infects his wife with HIV; this is not uncommon. Maybe he knows he's infected, but why would she want to use a condom? She also has her pressure from society, to bear a child.'

It's some of the men who are among the 15 per cent who didn't succumb to societal pressure to marry, or, like Singh Gohil, escaped unhappy marriages, that we're off to meet now.

In 2011, Singh Gohil inaugurated his latest project under the auspices of the Lakshya Trust: a retirement home for gay men and third genders that he's named, somewhat awkwardly, Janet, after the late American donor who made the project possible.

Cutting through a green counterpane of farmed fields, we arrive in Hanmenteshwar village, a sleepy commune on the banks of the Narmada river a couple of hours out of Rajpipla. It is here that Janet can accommodate 50 retired gay men and hijras.

We walk through the door into a whitewashed space with a river view, where a handful of men sit around, some talking, some staring at the river with rheumy eyes, some sipping tea. Heads crane inquisitively as our group walks in.

'Old-age care in India is centred round the traditional family,' explains Singh Gohil as we take a seat next to one man, who's dressed neatly in white pyjamas. 'There's little state retirement support in our country, so children are an Indians' insurance against old age. But gays and third genders are often ostracised by their families, like this man next to us. He has had no family for over 40 years. So where is his safety net? Where does he go when he's old and weak?

The guranas have been broken. I saw a desperate need for something like this.'

Deepak asks the man to recount his story. He's perhaps in his late 70s, his cropped and hennaed haircut giving him more than a passing resemblance to a young Audrey Hepburn.

Deepak translates. 'His name is Rahul. He was the son, he says, of a rich Bengali family. But he doesn't talk to anyone in his family. He hasn't for 40 years.'

'Because they discovered he was gay?' I ask.

'Yes,' says Deepak. 'It was found that he had slept with a servant boy, so he was shunned. He joined the army for a while, moving from city to city; he was always running, he says. Now he is old and tired. He says he has no energy to run.'

How many men does Singh Gohil expect to take up residence at Janet? As a conservative and undeveloped state, Gujarat is an interesting choice for such a project.

'At the moment we have as many Western men showing interest, which surprises me,' he says. 'We have two men coming to join us from France soon. I don't think the location is a problem, if we are a family.'

Singh Gohil lets the word 'family' play across his lips. He smiles.

'Yes, I've created my own gay and third-sex family. This gay family keeps me alive because of the amount of love I've received. They've always supported me during my bad times, through emotional turmoil, and through happy times. This motivates me to work more for the community and welfare of our people. I have no family now. We – the hijras, homosexuals, whatever we are – are my family now.'

8 | PA'S SIX-PACK, Amritsar

Getting pumped in the Punjab

Indian police are being paid to grow moustaches because bosses believe it makes them command more respect. Ten policemen in the northern state are already receiving 30 rupees every month for their efforts. The district police told BBC News: 'Moustaches are improving the personalities of our constables. They are acquiring an aura of their own. They are creating a positive impression on the local people and getting a lot of respect. It takes time to keep a proper moustache. A good one has to take a turn near the angle of the upper lip,' he added. Men in rural India have traditionally sported impressive moustaches to assert their masculinity.

—*BBC News*

It's 5 o'clock in the morning, as I bundle aboard an Express train headed north, packed with well-to-do Sikhs en route to the Sikh religion's holiest religious site, the Golden Temple at Amritsar.

My journey to this Punjabi city that's an hour across the border from the Pakistani second city of Lahore (and thus secondarily famous for the bloodiest events of Indian Partition) apparently coincides with a festival relating to Guru Nanak, the founder member of Sikhism, that youngest of the subcontinent's major religions. This, I realise, accounts for the obscene crush of bodies in every train carriage. Yet festival crowds are a common encounter in this nation of daily festivals and – unfazed – I'd settled into a pleasant six-hour elbow-to-elbow journey beside a family of Sikhs on weekend pilgrimage.

The family, three teenagers and their middle-aged parents, were in the company of their nephew, a software engineer based in San Francisco. Plump and wired into pocketsful of techie gadgets, he had picked up the American affectation of hygiene obsession during his years on the West Coast and, as a wallah handed around thermoses of coffee and biscuits in envelopes embossed with an Indian rail logo, had muttered loudly about 'improved sanitary requirements'.

I'd decided to add Amritsar to my itinerary as I'd heard so much about its men. Having touched on the world of the gay man and the hijra, I wanted to investigate the supposed apogee of Indian manhood, the Punjabi male. My Delhi friend Akshaya hadn't been the first to lionise the majesties of this creature: I knew that the Victorian British felt an affinity with the Sikh and Muslim 'warrior races', focusing their distaste on the 'mild' Hindu and 'effeminate and degenerate' Bengali. A photographer acquaintance honed the focus. 'It's not all Punjabi men. It's Punjabi Sikhs,' he'd said, plying me with brandies and Marlboro Lights, and making no secret of the fact he was exploring his own Punjabi Sikh potency by staring at my legs.

'It's our broad chests and warrior bloodline. It's our swords and turbans too. I know for a fact that Scandinavian women find Sikh turbans erotic. Most white women do. Look at Punjab, that strapping Sikh Sardar who saves Annie in *Annie*: fantasy man!' he added.

The Punjab's rich soils supply the subcontinent's tallest soldiers, its toughest Kabaddi wrestlers and its long-distance truckers, who famously ply the old Grand Trunk Road from Peshawar to Delhi in painted trucks bearing the legend 'Jat on Prowl' (thanks to such stunts the Jats are often, perhaps unfairly, blamed by Delhiites for backward male attitudes impinging on that city from the rural north).

Punjab is also the cradle of Indian bodybuilding, one of the most visible expressions of Punjabi machismo. Everywhere in Amritsar posters of rippling bodybuilders vie with those of movie stars, advertising the highest number of gyms per capita in India, with names such as Big Guns!, Wow! and King's.

I'm without Dimple and have enlisted Gobind as my guide. Five years ago, he was a young bodybuilder hotly tipped for fame, but he was forced to stop working out after an episode of 'roid rage', the nickname for the bouts of out-of-the-blue aggression that are the side effect of hormone doping. Still, 28-year-old Gobind remains well connected in the bodybuilding world, and we now find ourselves heading off in a black-and-yellow cab to an appointment at an under-the-counter supplements and steroids store belonging to one of his contacts.

Rajesh, the proprietor of Pumped, is running me through his daily diet. 'Glutamine, five grams in water at 7 a.m.; whey supplement at eight; three slices of brown bread; one black coffee with no sugar; then protein powder in milk. At 11 a.m. I get my breakfast: three boiled potatoes and a little bit of paneer. Then at 12 o'clock a scoop and a half of protein shake; two o'clock five eggs, plus five brown bread and two bananas. Then, before I work out, two energiser powders dissolved in water, then, after workout, five sweet potatoes, and 1 kg of boiled chicken...'

I look around his small store. It's stacked with row upon row of imported supplement powders in black 10kg packs, like a film noir Manhattan skyline, though the supporting cast is more Miami Beach: four strapping men in muscle vests and micro T-shirts, ranged around the small floor space like abandoned inflatables at high tide. I wonder what the room's aroma will be like later on, in the full-wattage heat of mid-afternoon; it's noon and already pungent.

'Is all of this expensive?' I ask.

'Yes, lakhs of rupees in a year to do it right,' says Rajesh. 'And the government gives no financial support. In the UK and US they give money to bodybuilders. And the injections are expensive: 80 to 90 thousand rupees for two mil that you need two times a week.'

As in most countries, steroid use is banned in India. Still, the hormones integral to the bodybuilding habit are readily had, albeit as inflated in price as their users' pecs. After a sidelong glance out the window, Rajesh produces a box of vials the size of a carry-on suitcase.

Gobind talks me through them. There are esters of testosterone with various uses: for bulking cycles, or for cutting cycles, the latter when you're preparing for competition and want to keep muscle mass while shedding fat. There's Winistrol, the king of steroids that promises muscle mass, stamina and 'great pumps', but also leads to acne and stiff joints; and Dianabol, a perennial favourite on the US scene that boosts users' weight-lifting prowess, but also leads to body bloating. Then the most notorious of all anabolics, Deca Durabolin, an injectable steroid first popularised in the 1970s. It's the bulker par excellence, promoting the 'Schwarzenegger look' of 40lb of muscle gain over a few months, but also the unwelcome side effect of 'Deca Dick'.

'Basically, you get a limpy,' says Gobind. 'That's why you have to balance it with the testosterone.'

Rajesh is beginning to look woebegone, so I ask him and his neighbour Vish, a bulked-out 5 ft 4 in with a cuboid look, who first inspired them to take to the weights.

'Salman Khan,' they growl in unison.

Khan is Hindi cinema's self-appointed 'bad boy'. The veteran of 80 Bollywood movies, he first ripped his shirt off in 1989's smash *Maine Pyar Kiya*, or 'I Fell in Love', a tale of desire across the class divide in which millionaire's son Prem (Khan) falls for Suman, the daughter of a poor mechanic. In the signal sequence, a mullet-haired Khan peels off his shirt as Suman simpers at his ankles, exposing an exotic landscape of gleaming muscles above the high waist of snow-washed jeans. *Maine Pyar Kiya* was a landmark in Bollywood, giving wings to the current weightlifting trend and inspiring a recursive conceit.

Indeed, shirt loss became such a staple of Khan's oeuvre that directors were driven to ever-camper plot mechanisms to liberate him from his outer garments. In *Wanted* (2009) fire burns the offending item to a crisp; in 2010's *Dabaang* a rogue gust does the job; whereas in *Bodyguard* from 2011 a spurt of water renders Khan topless and beaded with droplets.

In the two decades since the first film's release many Bollywood actors have followed Khan's lead, including SRK, who got buff for 2007 smash *Om Shanti Om*, and a flurry of musclemen who achieved fame purely on the strength of their chiselled assets, such as Prateik Babbar and Guatam Rode. The trend also inspired salivating Bollywood blog ShirtlessBollywoodMen.

'The best one was where Salman's a rock star and he rips off his shirt on stage when he's playing guitar,' muses Rajesh.

Ten minutes later we're en route to a gym on the outskirts of town that's run by one of Rajesh's friends – Onkar, a local who, like many successful Punjabi businessmen, juggles multiple business ventures, from gyms to hotels and the staging of beauty contests.

Sitting on the back seat of a cab between two bodybuilders, I suddenly feel like I did when, aged 7, I was trapped in a Spanish elevator with a man grappling a large lilo. I'm relieved when we pull up in a suburb 45 minutes' drive from downtown Amritsar. Visually, it's a sleepy city enclave: dogs spreading out on the warm pavement, occasionally batting off a tick; housewives lumbering home under bags of channa flour; groups of young men standing around cleaning their teeth with pocket knives, spitting between their feet, shooting the breeze.

But aurally, it's off kilter. The street quakes with the gurgling bass and bravura rantings of gangsta rap. The culprit's our destination: Onka's gym, a squat building with full-drop glass windows in which 20 or so male bodies can be seen, curling weights; pressing barbells, their faces red with exertion; admiring themselves in the mirrors that ring the room.

Standing around the perimeter of this peculiar glass box are a handful of slight teenage males, trying to make themselves invisible in shaded corners, behind masks of acne. I'm the only woman in, or anywhere near, this testosterone-fuelled joint, and I feel self-conscious as Onka takes me on a tour of the sights. I'm glad I've worn a modest, mustard-coloured shalwaar kameez for the occasion.

As we pass the more pumped-up males, Gobind enjoins them to tense their biceps, or instructs me to look at them doing their 'craps'.

'Craps? Craps? What craps?' I say, alarmed.

'You know, "craps"... "cur-raaps".'

'Curl reps?'

'Yessss! Cur-raaaps!'

We step up to the office to share bananas and sticky protein shakes with the man Gobind addresses as 'Onks'.

'What do the women think of your look?' I ask Onka. 'Do Punjabi women go for it?'

'Of course,' says Gobind quickly. 'Punjabi women love men with muscles.'

In fast Punjabi, huffing with exertion as he speaks as if he's pressing 40 lb, Onka joins in.

Gobind translates. 'He says women like them. Big men make them feel, you know, like women. Punjabi women are real women and they like their Punjabi men to be real men.'

The protein shakes are drained and everyone's looking a little embarrassed. Gobind and I are about to leave the men to their craps when I notice something flickering on the wall. It's the sort of mini-shrine you'd find in an Indian home, with offerings of jasmine flowers, sweets, votive candles and incense sticks arrayed around the crude figure of a black-faced deity.

'Who's that?' I ask.

'It's Hanuman, the monkey god,' says Gobind. 'He's the deity of all bodybuilders and wrestlers.'

'There's a god of bodybuilding?' I wonder.

'Yes. Hanuman is a symbol of strength and energy. He can move mountains, seize the clouds and match Vishnu's bird, Garuda, in his speed of flight. The Hanuman cult is getting big now because of all the bodybuilders. There's a festival in Bihar called Hanuman Jayanti, where wrestlers and bodybuilders play games of strength. Rajesh goes this year. They fast all day and wear a tilak of orange sindoora from Hanuman's body on their forehead, for good luck. Then they balance big rocks on their chest and pull cars – like, a jeep, say – with their teeth.'

I can't help smiling at this image, though nobody else seems to be. I also can't help wondering why, in a land so long prized for its manly males, so many of them feel the need to big themselves up.

PART THREE: THE EAST

It's different out east

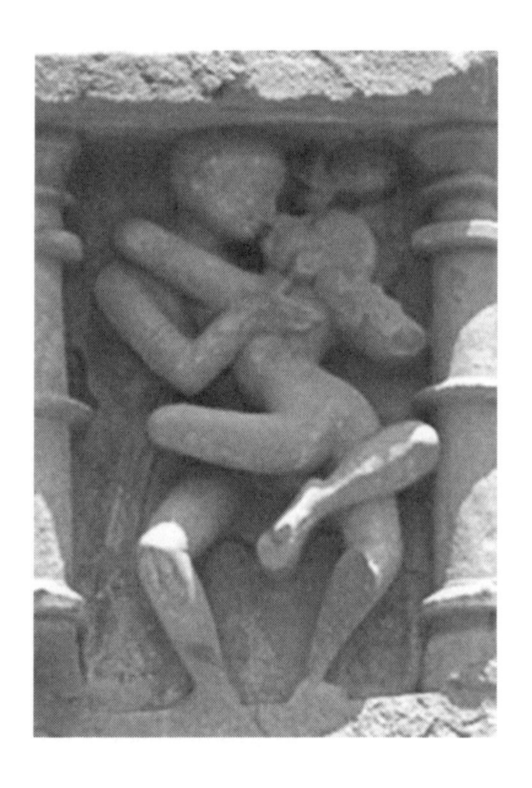

9 | MA'S FIVE HUSBANDS, Meghalaya

Another India, where women rule

A man should treat a woman according to the nature of the region she comes from. The women of central India are mostly noble women with pure habits; they hate kissing, scratching and biting, and so do the women of Bahlika and Avantika, though they are fond of unusual sexual acts. Women from Malava and Abhira like embracing, kissing, scratching, biting and sucking, and although they do not like to be wounded they can be won over by slaps. The women who live in the land watered by the Indus and other five rivers like oral sex. The women of the West and Lata are capable of fierce sexual energy, and they moan softly.

In the land where women rule, and in Kosala, the women like to be slapped hard and generally use sex tools, for their sexual energy is very rough indeed.

—Kama Sutra, Book Two, On Sexual Union

The state of Meghalaya is very different from the India we've come from. A pine-wooded outpost bordered by Bangladesh to the south and Bhutan and Myanmar to the north and east, the state owes more to the latter two than to the great teardrop of India to which it is tethered, awkwardly, by a spur of land between Kathmandu and Bangladesh. We'd seen the land unspreading from above, a voluptuous tapestry of green and snow-capped peaks, as we'd flown into the airport.

Topographically and climatically, Meghalaya is distinct to the sultry and populous Indian plains. There's the extraordinary rainfall, for starters. The state's lilting name is Sanskrit for 'abode of the clouds'; and Cherapunjee, a small town near to Meghalaya's southern border with Bangladesh, is the wettest place on earth, with an annual average rainfall of 12,000 mm and the world record for the wettest year in recorded history: 26,461 mm (1041.75 in), which fell on a Raj-era Cherapunjee between 1 August 1860 and 31 July 1861.

Meghalaya's Swiss chalet–like homes are battened down against this uncompromising drenching, with downturned corrugated iron roofs onto which converging southwest and northeast monsoonal rains thunder every year, from June through to September. Meghalaya's men, too, appear to be battened down, heads bowed in imported Chinese bobble-hats, tugged tightly over their ears.

The state's women eye the rains with insouciance. They pickle, dry and preserve foods to see them through the monsoon months; they rainproof their homes; they refuse to stint on style.

Meghalaya is home to three matrilineal tribes: the Garo (who come from Indo-Burmese stock), the Jaintia (thought to have come from the region that's now Bangladesh) and the Khasi (also the largest, with genetic links to the Cambodian Mon Khmer). Each of these tribes traces their bloodline from mother to daughter and distributes the bulk of the family inheritance, and certainly the family property, to the youngest daughter – in Khasi the khaduh or 'heiress' – who is thenceforth considered custodian of the family name and home. When the khaduh marries, her husband traditionally joins her in her kin home, or ing, to which he has no right of possession and, within which, little say over family decision making. And in the event of the khaduh's death, he is expected to return to his birth family's ing.

The most prominent of Meghalaya's tribes are the Khasi, who predominate in the city we'll stay in for the next five days: the Meghalayan capital, Shillong. Khasi women dress in the Jainsem and Dhara, wrap skirts and one-shouldered pinafores that give the body an elegant, column-like silhouette. It's a look, to most foreign eyes, that is bizarrely out of synch with this wild-flower-dotted hill community, like the *Vogue* fashion department arriving en masse in small-town Scotland.

The practice of matrilineal inheritance among the Khasi has lately become politicised, thanks to Syngkhong Rympei Thymmai (which loosely translates as 'Home Hearth Restructured'), an increasingly vocal Khasi men's rights movement that is lobbying to reclaim what it sees as the lost glory of 'U Rangbah', the Khasi male, through reforms to Khasi inheritance laws and social mores.

Keith Pariat, president of Syngkhong Rympei Thymmai, makes for an unlikely grass-roots agitator. He's kindly looking, a late middle-aged man with expressive crinkles around his eyes, the outline of his vest clearly visible through his neatly ironed shirt.

We've arranged to meet him and other key SRT members at Earle Holiday Home, a hotel complex on the outskirts of Shillong city centre with an aquatic-themed novelty restaurant and canary yellow-painted entrance foyer. The latter's where we're seated now, on squeaky faux-leather easy chairs surrounded by plastic umbrella plants.

Pariat married a khaduh. His wife now runs the family's main business, a chain of general stores, while he manages his own small transportation company.

'When I married I left my father and mother's house to go to my wife's kin house,' he tells us. 'When a woman does this, as women do all over India, she can adapt: women are subtle and softly spoken... But men cannot adapt. I could not adapt. As husbands of khaduh we feel we are sidelined; as if all we are there for is to breed.

'For example,' he continues, without giving us pause to interject, 'I am only allowed to get involved in the family business at Christmas. Then my wife lets me dress the shop windows, because I have the artistic touch.'

I catch Dimple suppressing a smile at this, Pariat unselfconsciously echoing the complaints, common across the patriarchal world, of the undermined housewife. Dimple is seated across the foyer, beneath a framed 3D picture of plastic flowers and next to Rivertis Patriong, a Khasi lonely heart.

Rivertis is a 39-year-old seismological officer for the Indian government who hopes that the agitations of Syngkhong Rympei Thymmai will change Khasi society sufficiently to help him find a bride.

'Although I'm educated and have a great job, none of the local girls even look at me,' he complains. 'They all want to marry men from outside: white men, or men from [patriarchal] India, confident Marathi businessmen, who come in and take over all of the Khasi property.'

'He's the victim, the victim!' Pariat interrupts vigorously. 'The Khasi girls don't respect us. They want to marry outsiders. There was a study last year by the Meghalaya Women's Commission of Khasi girls of marriageable age. 100 per cent said they would prefer to marry a man from outside rather than a Khasi man – 100 per cent!'

'Why?' asks Dimple, looking unconvinced.

'Well, they think that Khasi men are useless,' Pariat explains. 'And partly they are right. Many of our young men who marry will let their wives shoulder all responsibility and enjoy life. They'll impregnate another Khasi girl, or turn to drink. There's more money about now, so they can get tight on imported whisky. And this is our fault.' He leans forward, putting his shirt-sleeved elbows on his knees as he extemporises.

'It is the fault of our weak, matrilineal society. We of Syngkhong Rympei Thymmai say that men must rule. We are more emotionally stable. We are not hysterical like women. And we say that unless men become the first sex we will go extinct!'

The next morning the sun rises over muesli-packet mountain views as Dimple and I breakfast on small, densely sweet Cherapunjee oranges. She's been clamouring to get her hands on this delicacy, one of Meghalaya's key exports into southern India, along with pungent turmeric and bharat lalokia, a chilli-based preserve that advertises itself as 'the world's most potent pickle'.

We're sitting on wrought-iron chairs in guesthouse grounds modelled on an English country garden: brick paths, rambling roses, fleshy foxgloves and snapdragons in explosive bloom.

'Pariat's theory about hysteria reminded me of something,' says Dimple, picking up a red, bullet-shaped sour fruit – another of Meghalaya's specialities that, like ja-snam (rice cooked in pigs' blood), fails to find many takers beyond the state borders. She nibbles a corner, and winces.

'Meghalaya was where they used to send the English ladies during the Raj. There were sanatoria here run by the missions. The idea was that the fresh air and high altitudes would cure these women of the hysteria that came upon them in the Indian heat.'

Dimple has a theory about hysteria, as she tells me now, through a mouthful of orange segments. 'We saw hysteria with the Victorian Britons, and we see the same now with Indian women. Hysteria is what women do when they're suppressed, isn't it?

'Indian women are the world's biggest hypochondriacs: we can't breathe one minute; another minute we're dying of a dramatic illness. Like those British ladies with their fainting couches. Looking back, I used to be like that. It was the only way I could protest against my fate, my traditional husband and my controlling mother-in-law. I'd become ill and take myself to bed.'

Later that day we have an appointment with two successful Khasi 30-something businesswomen, for their take on the crisis afoot in Meghalayan matriarchy. Lisa and Mary are close friends, bonded by their saucy sense of humour and a resignation, as modern Khasi women who have grown to despise Khasi men, to permanent singlehood.

We meet at Mary's mother's ing. The property's a spacious gated bungalow on the outskirts of Shillong decorated with floral curtains and carefully polished ornaments. In these mumsy surroundings, Mary and Lisa strike an incongruous note, downing their half-glasses of whisky and chain-smoking Camel Lights. They lower their voices every time a girl servant, who's preparing a supper of fish in sesame paste, rice in blood and smoked dried pork, anxiously enters the room. Dinner is already two hours late and the whisky's going rapidly to my head. It must be the mountain air.

'Keith and his followers are all doom and gloom, you know,' says Lisa.

'But Khasi men don't have it too bad, really. The Karo tribes traditionally kidnap the man the tribeswoman wants as a husband; and the Jaintia tribes, they bring husbands in for procreation and nothing more. My grandma had five husbands. Only the women really know who the father of their child is, and the way I see it, that's how it should be.'

Behind me, on a doily-dotted pine bookshelf, I notice a stack of DVDs. I'm surprised to see that they include complete series of the vampire-themed fantasy romance *Twilight* and the Abba movie *Mamma Mia!*. I ask about them.

'Now Colin Firth,' says Mary. 'That's my kind of man.'

'Yes,' says Lisa luxuriantly, 'verrrrrrrry dishy.'

So they would consider dating a white man, I ask, hearing my stomach rumble and glancing towards the open kitchen door, from where an enraged crescendo of clattering pans drifts towards us.

'Yes,' says Mary quickly, frowning at the noise. 'It's most Khasi girls' ambition. My grandfather was a white man – a Britisher. So there's a tradition there. Despite what Pariat and his nuts say, most Khasi girls wouldn't marry an Indian man. They know what it means.'

At this she closes her fists and crosses her wrists over each other, to indicate handcuffs.

'So,' I ask, 'you've given up on any prospect of romance with a Khasi man?'

Mary nods ruefully and lights another Camel. 'Well, would you find our men sexy: workless… shiftless?'

Her complaint reminds me of US author Hanna Rosin's 2012 book *The End of Men*, which portrays the power shift between the genders in working-class America. In Rosin's portrait of the state of that nation, a quasi-apocalyptic one, women are 'plastic' workers adapting to the new realities of a communications economy, raising children alone as single mothers. Working-class American males are 'cardboard men', floundering after the demise of the manufacturing jobs they relied on for their income and sense of identity.

In some quarters the book was presented as a triumph for women, the dawn of the Age of Aquarius and the promise of feminism bearing fruit. However, I can't help but see all of these scrapheaped males and overstretched women as a tragedy – a tragedy of self-worth and identity that's opening an unbreachable chasm between the sexes among working-class Westerners, as it has among the Khasi.

But then, some attempts to reawaken Western men's self-worth smack, as the campaigns of the Khasi do, of an attempt to reintroduce patriarchy by the back door. I ask Lisa and Mary whether they've heard of that US phenomenon the Surrendering Movement. Popularised in the US in the early noughties, Surrenderists are part of the Second Wave feminist backlash. They propose, in books such as the *Surrendered Single* and the seminal *The Surrendered Wife*, by 'former shrew' Laura Doyle, that women are happiest when they obey their husbands at all times; that they should submit to sex whenever their husbands wish; and that they should forgive indiscretions away from home.

It's an uncomfortable thought, I put to Lisa and Mary, but is it the case that male dominance is an essential part of the architecture of male–female relationships; at the very least the basis of good sex? Is power – or rather, as the ancient Greeks understood, a power imbalance – integral to sexual attraction?

'Hah! Nooo way,' says Lisa hotly, one eye on Colin Firth. 'I cannot imagine why a thinking, self-respecting woman would live that way, and a Western woman too, a Western woman who doesn't know how lucky she is! Keeping the peace at home would be a likely explanation, I suppose, but I would never subject myself to such a sad life.'

Mary, Lisa, Dimple and I repair to the table bedecked with a floral tablecloth for our long-awaited meal. Dimple looks happier than I've seen her in a long time, liberated somehow from the anxiety that she shoulders, like a damp chadoor, when she's at home in Delhi.

I glance around the table and ask myself who's the luckiest of us four: Dimple, striving for her modern life in a recalcitrant patriarchal India, with her network of servants to ease her struggle? Mary and Lisa, self-possessed and powerful, but deprived of male companionship? Or me, the Westerner, juggling the choices of a post-1960s world, aware that my generation feels cheated by the unrealised promises – both romantic and economic – of Second Wave feminism?

It's not an easy call.

10 | SEX, DEATH AND SPIRITUAL KICKS, Varanasi

Meeting the Aghoris – sex, death and the forbidden as a route to liberation

We gave her everything we owned just to sit at her table
Just a smile would lighten everything
Sexy Sadie she's the latest and the greatest of them all.
She made a fool of everyone.
Sexy Sadie.

—Lyrics to 'Sexy Sadie (AKA Maharishi Mahesh Yogi)', written by John Lennon in India, 1968, credited to Lennon–McCartney

In London, before departing on my Indian sexploration, I'd sunk a good bottle of red with 63-year-old Nick Black. Now a sailor and indie movie director with a mid-Atlantic drawl, as a young man Black had lived the baby boomer dream to the psychedelic letter.

He recalled his 22nd birthday. 'I spent it in the courtyard of a Tantric art collector in Bangalore, smoking hashish with 40 naked shaivite sannyasi covered in mud. Arione DeWinter, Petra and Ira from the Living Theatre were there:

chains, leather, you name it. Mad as fuck. I think we had our own cult.'

It was the early 1970s and Black was following the youth-cultural mood: a mood that was looking both easterly and to the occult, from the teachings of Victorian occultist Aleister Crowley, or the GreatBeast666, to the Himalayan Ashram of 'spiritual adviser to the Beatles' Maharishi Mahesh Yogi, to the beaches of Goa, fast becoming a counter-cultural outpost of self-appointed 'Freaks', and the 'buddhafield' at Pune, run by the provocative guru Bhagwan Shree Rajneesh, or Osho.

By the mid-1970s, Osho operated out of his sprawling ashram east of Bombay funded by Greek shipping heiress Catherine Venizelos (or Ma Yoga Mukta, as she was renamed). The ashram hosted 30,000 visitors a year, with 15,000 permanent orange robe-clad sannyasins ('renouncers'), predominantly Europeans and Americans. In what's been described as a 'madhouse carnival atmosphere', Osho's disciples undertook experimental therapy sessions, which explored physical aggression and unfettered sexual encounters between participants.

Controversy soon dogged Osho's centre, however. In 1974, Beat Generation veteran Dick Price claimed to have exited the ashram with a broken arm following a period of eight hours locked in a room with participants armed with wooden weapons. It was also alleged that Osho's Western sannyasins were financing extended stays in India through prostitution and drug running, a few later saying that Osho gave these money-making stunts his blessing.

In May 1980, after an attempt was made on Osho's life by a young Hindu fundamentalist, the 'sex guru' moved his ashram from Pune to Oregon, in the US, where he encountered open hostility from the locals and expounded increasingly wonky end-of-the-world theories. He predicted that two-thirds of the world would die from AIDS, and that the only antidote would be to create a Noah's Ark of Rajneesh consciousness. Despite his earlier teachings of sexual permissiveness as a route to super-consciousness, and his many gay followers, in Oregon Osho became a virulent homophobe, declaring 'gay perversion' to be responsible for the creation of AIDS: 'As a homosexual, you are not even a human being... You have fallen from dignity.'

He was deported from the US in 1985, after he admitted that the commune leadership had poisoned 751 residents of The Dalles, Oregon, with salmonella in order to incapacitate the city's voting population so that their own candidates would win the 1984 Wasco County elections. When Osho died at Pune in 1990, he left a mixed legacy.

Nevertheless, Osho's teachings on the importance of love, celebration, creativity and humour strike a chord with many young Indians, as do his views on the dangers of the suppression of sex brought about by static belief systems. Today, the Osho International Meditation resort at Pune attracts 200,000 visitors a year.

Despite hearing colourful reports of Osho's sex-yoga, back in 1972 Black instead headed to the Himalayas to work on raising the coiled snake of his Kundalini. 'I tried, babe,' he told me. 'I tried for six months, but the Kundalini wasn't coming. So I decided this spiritual-sexual Eastern thing was junk. But the trouble for all of us – working-class kids, debs gone off the rails – was that, when it came to the ideas of our parents, it was game over...

'Once you'd had sex on LSD the chances you were going to go back to the sexual ethics of the Methodists or Puritans was near zero.'

Many of the spiritual thrill seekers of Black's generation headed to Goa, that palm-fringed state off the west of India where throughout the early 1970s a bacchanalian atmosphere held sway among a clique who called themselves 'the Goa Freaks'.

Cleo Odzer was among them. For a year a devotee of Osho at Pune, later Odzer, who was born to a rich Jewish family in Manhattan, would become an archetypical Goa Freak.

Before her death, aged 50, from AIDS in 2001, she spoke to filmmaker Marcus Robbin about her life in the 1970s, for his melancholic documentary *Last Hippie Standing*:

> *We were all freaks. There weren't any tourists at that time. It was just this group of freaks; naked. And to be naked is to be free: there was so such a freedom in being naked on the beach... There was such a harmony with the palm trees.*

This freedom, as she describes it in her book *Goa Freaks: My Hippie Years in India*, extended to open sex on the beach and LSD-fuelled 'transcendental' orgies.

Despite Odzer's talk of the freedom she felt to explore the outer limits of the hippies' sex and drug taking in India's sunshine state, this state of affairs incensed Goa's Christian communities. Odzer's cine-film footage of the early 1970s shows the Freaks openly taking drugs in front of young local beach children. And, as an old-timer I once met in Goa put it to me, 'Imagine how the Catholic nuns felt about the orgies and nudity and rumours of hippy waifs breastfeeding monkeys. Not "far-out", that's for sure.'

And so, in much the way that the San Francisco 1967 Summer of Love mutated into a city benighted by drug addiction and crime by the waning days of that decade, the Goa Freak idyll was distorted into a bacchanalia of summer drug binges and monsoon-month drug runs to support the Freaks' extravagant habits. By 1979, Odzer was running a drug den on the beach at the Freaks' Goa stronghold of Anjuna, as she told Robbin:

> *I called it 'Anjuna Dragoona Saloona'. And I would sell hash and cocaine and heroin. And it started out as something really beautiful. But some people started to fix... to inject drugs. People got so hungry for the drug, and we didn't have enough money. They had to inject it... So I split the house in two, and I had the people who were injecting on the second floor, and the people who were smoking and snorting on the ground floor. And somebody called it a 'shooting gallery'. And I never heard that expression before, and I said 'Oh, how cute; a shooting gallery!' So in this way [many users] died. And a lot of people made mistakes because, with the heroin, you get lazy. 'Uh, I should check on this, but no, I'm too lazy to check on this'. So they go to jail, they ended up in jail. Ultimately, our society died.*

The third outpost on this 1960s and 1970s hippy circuit was India's holiest city, Varanasi, otherwise known as Benares. For several months in the 1970s, former Beatle George Harrison occupied a hotel overlooking one of the ghats, or ancient stairways leading down to the Ganges. Here he studied Hindu scripture, practised the sitar (having studied under Ravi Shankar in Bombay) and gathered material for what would become his 1974 album, *Festival of India*.

'The Ganges, the Ganga, this is where they all come,' says our guide Aram, an anthropology lecturer, as Dimple and I step out of an autorickshaw and into Kashi, the shadowy and aromatic old centre of this, the oldest continuously inhabited city on earth.

'Goldie Hawn comes here every year and takes up a room overlooking the Holy River. George Harrison had his ashes scattered here. This is the Mother River, the embodiment of Shakti, the water that takes up the Hindu dead and, in doing so, it's said, let's loose their souls in the state of moksha.

'Look at it this way,' he continues, talking through teeth reddened by a betel leaf–chewing habit, 'there are 8.4 million possibilities for your next reincarnation – from all the life in the sea to cockroaches and politicians. So, for some, earth is hell in this life, and for some, earth is heaven. Moksha is the escape from this cycle of birth and rebirth. It is the release of the soul.'

If, as a Hindu, you make it to Kashi – on your own legs, on a stretcher when you're gasping your last, or as a pot of ashes carried by your family members – moksha is pretty much in the bank. If you die at Varanasi, Hindus believe, release from the cycle of reincarnation is a double-seal guarantee. This belief accounts for the proliferation of hospices in Varanasi; and the regular sight of ailing people trailing catheters and oxygen supplies as they shuffle aboard buses, planes and trains bound for this northeast Indian city.

In addition to tourists, moribund Hindus and Westerners on spiritual quests, Varanasi attracts holy men in their multitudes: from nomad ascetics who wander the hills, to showy gurus hoping to make a rupee by attracting Western devotees, in the tradition of Osho and Maharishi.

Most notorious among these holy men at Varanasi are the Aghors, or Aghori, an enigmatic group that I'm here to meet. They are itinerant Tantric Hindu sadhus who make a point of embracing the grotesque and forbidden as a route to the divine. The Aghors live on the many smouldering cremation grounds in this city of death. They eat from human skulls; sometimes, it is said, even human flesh. To the modern Indian middle classes, the Aghors' reputation is vampiric, something between Count Dracula and a campy Halloween drag act; part theatre, but part feared.

A Delhi academic explained the Aghori philosophy to me by phone, as Dimple and I boarded a plane for the city, alongside a cabin full of elderly and ailing Hindus, at Lucknow airport. I was interested, in particular, in finding out about the Aghors' unusual attitude to sex.

'Ah, Aghors,' he said, with a dark laugh, 'they are very interesting, the Aghors. They think boundaries to mortal existence should be explored as a road to the divine: sex and death form these boundaries. So when it comes to sex and death, the Aghors have no taboos. And this in a religion, Hinduism, that's based, of course, on its taboos.'

The Aghors' ideas of an intersection between sex and death reminded me of that famous French metaphor for orgasm, *le petit mort* or little death. It also called to mind that idea of a commingling of sex and the occult that so appealed to the hippies on their sex and spirituality quests; the idea, too, of sex used as a medium to the divine.

'The Aghors have their reputation, and certainly they like to shock,' Aram says, as we board a wooden boat, or bajra, at a ghatside awriggle with South Korean and American tourists. Dimple treads gingerly between cowpats onto the bajra's wooden slats. She's a little squeamish about Varanasi after, during her last trip here, being poked in the shoulder and turning around to discover that her assailant was the arm of a dead man, hanging off a stretcher bound for one of the hundreds of funeral pyres.

'They will drink urine in front of you. They will lick a leper. They wear black, which is a big no-no to Hindus and why you see so many bright colors in sarees,' Aram continues. 'But you have to understand that this is not just to shock. It is Shiva. To Aghors, Shiva is the route to moksha and everything is Shiva; specifically everything in this, the city of Shiva. That includes, most precisely, the things that to Hindus are taboos.'

We pull away from the ghat as a boat laden with camera-toting South Koreans lists into us, churning up a cumulus of the white plastic bags that bob on the bouillon-brown waters near the shore.

'These taboos are the five Ms,' Aram continues, as the boat steadies. 'Fish eating, or matsya, is forbidden, and animal flesh eating, or māṃsa. Wine, or madya, of course; and the eating of parched grains, which is an old idea about the purity of food. And the big one: sex, or maithu.'

The Aghors' attitude to sex strikes me as at odds with the asceticism espoused by most Indian holy men. Hindu sadhus are typically defined by their physical self-denial, most colourfully seen in the case of their extreme feats of physical privation, such as Amar Bharati, the sadhu who's famously kept his right arm raised above his head since 1973.

In Ashrama, the delineation of the four ideal stages of Hindu life, sexual abstinence features prominently: at Bramacharya, the stage of student life to age 27, when strict chastity is viewed as the ideal; and at Sannyasa, the fourth or renunciation stage, when the Hindu withdraws from the world and renounces earthly pursuits.

Hindu scriptures prescribe the practice of Bramacharya (a word which came to mean chastity) for householders prior to important religious rites or observances. Of sadhus, or renunciates, a lifelong vow of Brahmacharya is often expected, to facilitate the devotee's surrender to their gurus or gods. For the most extreme practitioners of Bramacharya the term became conflated with the principle of refraining from the voluntary loss of semen.

In modern times the cult of sexual abstinence was famously espoused by Mohandas 'Mahatma' Gandhi. In *Intimate Relations: Exploring Indian Sexuality*, psychiatrist

Sudhir Kakar examines Gandhi's vow of celibacy through his lifelong correspondence. Before that vow, Gandhi admits he was a highly sexual and jealous husband to wife Kasturba Mohandas Gandhi, the daughter of a wealthy businessman to whom he was married by arrangement aged 14.

Gandhi's later renunciation of sex, Kakar suggests, can be traced back to his self-disgust around his father's death; an event that occurred when Kasturba and Gandhi were engaged in sexual intercourse in the next room. In his letters, this revulsion grows. Studying in England in his 20s, Gandhi is conflicted by his attraction to prostitutes and English girls. It is during his long sojourn in South Africa that he thinks of becoming celibate, while reading Tolstoy, the Russian novelist who proposed celibacy within marriage as the highest human state. Gandhi took the vow at 37 without consulting his wife.

In later life he went on to experiment with brands of vegetarian diet that would lessen the sexual urge and instructed girls as young as 12, including his great-niece Manu, to sleep naked next to him, in order to test the efficacy of his formulas.

'You know, you are honoured,' says Aram, as we step gingerly onto a ghat step that's sheening with wet fungal growth. 'This is my very last boat trip for the year. Come the monsoon and the bodies start bobbing up and some guides still go out, but I can't. You see, the city forbids the tipping of dead bodies in the river, but they still row out and dump in all those persons religion tells us we cannot burn: pregnant women and children, lepers, people killed by snakebite. And parts of bodies also: the limbs of the bodies whose families couldn't afford the wood to burn the body properly.

'I took a boat trip of tourists out late in the season two years ago,' he continues ruefully. 'And we saw one: a lady, her body all ghostly and bloated. She was pregnant. I relived it in my dreams for months. That's why I don't take boat tours in the monsoon.'

We pick our way up the ghat, past a young Indian tourist wearing bright green slacks and a T-shirt bearing the slogan 'Forget girlfriends: They get on your chest'.

'The last time I brought a woman to meet this Aghor, Sri Nath, it was a mixed success,' Aram now admits. 'She was desperate to conceive. He told her to go screw herself and that her mother was a donkey. Then he told her to climb up a hill on her knees praising Shiva. But, you see she did conceive!'

As for many Indian holy men, ad hoc fertility services are one of the Aghors' main income streams, alongside casting out demons and curing illness.

Sri Nath licks his sharp incisors as he takes us in. His limbs and great beehive of a dreadlock are caked in blue-white ash. At his feet is the ceremonial Aghor skull bowl, in his hand a staff with a skull-shaped handle and by his side, two young acolytes, who look to be in an advanced state of inebriation.

He growls something unintelligible.

'He's asking us what we want,' translates Aram.

Sri Nath, too, looks tipsy. Like many of the Varanasi-based sadhus, the Aghors are prone to substance abuse: the traditional bhang and chillum and – increasingly – alcohol and white powders, the latter the result of the sadhus' decades-long intermingling with the Western hippy and backpacker culture.

'To ask him a few questions about his life,' I assert, with a solicitous smile.

Sri Nath belches as Aram translates the request back to him. Dimple and I flinch. With another crescendo belch, he shoots out his opened palm, onto which Aram counts 500 rupees in 100-bill denominations. Then, without waiting for a question, Sri Nath begins his jeremiad, prodding at the ground with his staff for emphasis. Aram translates.

'He says he is the emperor of the cremation ground. He eats the offerings left for the dead. He takes the shrouds from the dead bodies. Nothing frightens him. Not people, not death. Ash is his clothing, as Lord Shiva himself uses it. Aghors, who are his children, are bound to use it.

'He has this ceremonial skull, which he searched the banks of the Ganga for. Afterwards, he pounded out the flesh of the skull. Now he eats and drinks from that same skull. He has no disgust. If he has hate and disgust, how would he share his food with dogs and eat from cremation grounds?'

Sri Nath lustily draws breath, before continuing.

'At night he says people are scared of the funeral grounds. That's when Sri Nath meditates undisturbed. He eats whatever is put in his bowl; maybe faeces; maybe human flesh. When the spirit is in him he would even drag a whole corpse off the pyre and eat it.'

Sri Nath takes a generous hit of chillum, supplied by an attendant to his left, and falls silent. It's a silence loaded with the implication that we should hand over another sheath of rupees.

'What about sex?' I ask, after a minute's wait. 'Does he follow the Aghori path of sex as a route to Shiva?'

'He says that now he has no greed or no lust, like he has no clocking on to work,' translates Aram. 'When he was a younger Aghor he would have sex, with prostitutes. He would seek out sex considered dirty by other Hindus: sex for example with women who were menstruating... prostitutes who were menstruating. He would live among the prostitutes; to him they were the same as all women. To him there was no disgust, and no taboo. To him, all is Shiva.'

'Did he ever have sex in the cremation grounds?' I ask. 'Or is this a myth about the Aghors?'

'Yes,' says Aram. 'This is the ritual sex practice of the Aghors: to have sexual intercourse with a menstruating woman in a graveyard at nighttime. It is a Tantric act. The woman is smeared in ashes from the graveyard and other Aghors will read mantras and beat drums.

'He says he is too old for the graveyard sex ritual now,' continues Aram, as Dimple looks on wide-eyed.

'He is complaining that it is difficult, even at night, to find peace and quiet at the cremation grounds to practise the Aghori rituals. Too many tourists, he says.'

We found out more about graveyard sex when we spoke to Ashok, the leader of the Kena Ram Baba moderate Aghori sect, a mild-mannered man dressed in a powder-blue 1970s-style safari suit.

Dimple, Aram and I meet Ashok at Varanasi's Kena Ram Baba Aghori Temple, entering the complex through an arch decorated with a daisy chain of human skulls. Inside, the temple is ranged around an exhibit in a glass box, which we view as we wait for Ashok. The oddest is a model exhibit of great Aghori leader Kena Ram Baba (who died in 1992) on his magic flying carpet. As we wait for Ashok to arrive, Dimple asks a temple guide why the current leader doesn't require the magic carpet for his own use.

'Because it might hit the airplanes,' the guide tells us, with no further explanation, before he pads off to retrieve Ashok.

'You see, the Aghors believe that orgasm and sex in the company of the dead will give rise to superpowers,' Ashok says.

As we drive him to another centre run by the sect, a hospital across the Ganges on the outskirts of town, he expounds on the Aghori sex ritual.

'It is believed that when this ritual involves sex with menstruating women the superpower sexual energy is released more effectively,' he says. 'One aspect of this ritual is that there has to be no force involved, and the woman has to take an equal part in the ritual, which is usually done in the dead of night. The ritual is elaborate and lasts for over an hour, from the time of undressing of the woman in the centre of the graveyard to the final act and orgasm. Aghors believe it is the duty of the man to delay orgasm until the ritual is completed.

'A few decades ago, in the hippy era, many foreigners came to the Aghori centres in Varanasi. They thought they could use the ritual sex practices for ESP [extra-sensory perception].'

A short time later and we've arrived at a squat white building bordered by a white fence. We enter the building to an unexpected scene: a plant-pot-scattered courtyard that could pass for a boutique hotel rather than a hospital. It's ringed by simple whitewashed rooms.

'So this is what I wanted to show you of the Aghors,' says Aram, as Ashok smiles in kindly approval. 'To show how their idea of embracing Hindu taboos can come to some good. This is Kust Seva Aghor Ashram. I first came here 15 years ago. It was a day that I will remember always. There were VIPs visiting Bihar at the time and, as many states do, the political cronies had run all of the beggars and lepers out of town with force, so the streets were clean for these VIPs.

'After many hundreds of miles of walking, over 200 lepers had arrived here at Benares, hearing they'd receive welcome. Many of them had never received any medical treatment and were in advanced states of the illness. I was one of the young volunteers who came to care for them, relieve their suffering as we could. Many died in front of us. I will never forget it.'

'Only a few lepers remain here now,' says Ashok. 'But when we set up as an ashram in the 1960s there were many, many lepers. These were the decades after independence and the Indira Gandhi State of Emergency, and there were few medical facilities, and most of the hospitals that existed wouldn't treat lepers, due to the stigma.

'But we Aghors,' he continues, beaming with pride. 'We Aghors would treat them!'

'They made it into the *Guinness Book of Records* in 1999,' adds Aram. 'They treated half a million lepers in 40 years... half a million!'

Ashok and his Aghori sect have been a reminder that for every fringe belief in Hindu spiritualism there's a moderate take on its teachings. Also, that the flipside to India's organisation of life via taboos – against sex, the eating of meat, the wearing of black – is, of course, an Indian tradition founded on facing down taboos, from sex to death and leprosy. Nowhere is this truer than in Varanasi, a city of approximately 23,000 temples dedicated (among the many to Shiva) to everyone from Annapurna, the goddess of food, to a giant temple to Hanuman, the monkey god we met back at Amritsar.

That night we take to the Ganges to experience another world record: Gunga Arti, a religious ritual-cum-party that's taken place at one of the Varanasi ghats, Dashashwamedh, every night for, Aram speculates, 'a thousand years'.

We reach Dashashwamedh just as this eternal party's starting. Crowds of upwards of a thousand have gathered on the ghat, mainly Indian pilgrims but also Westerners, the latter's broader backsides commanding two seats on the narrow spectator benches. In front of us, the Ganges shimmers in deep black, like liquid midnight.

Facing the river, and accompanied by the fluting tones of male temple singers, stand 15 novice priests, performing the Arti ritual.

'They face the Ganges as their deity,' Aram explains. 'They are getting immersed in the soul of the river, their eyes as their windows to the soul. Like the pop music songs say!'

In synchrony, the 15 young men wave lit ghee-candle wicks in figures of eight to the sky and river, leaving behind striations of bright light, like the tremulous after-trails of bonfire-night sparklers.

Behind us, on the banks of the ghat, are LED advertising hoardings. 'Love all. Serve all. Help ever, hurt never!' reads one, sponsored by the Bank of India; another, from an insurance company, reads, with an engaging typo: 'Without Water, Life is Dad!'

The temple singers sing gutsily. The crowd clap and chatter, sharing among themselves thermoses of chai. In the mid-distance I can make out smoke curling into the night sky from the ever-lit funeral pyres. It's a stirring scene, perhaps one of the world's most enduring celebrations of life, in this city that celebrates death.

As Gunga Arti draws to a close, Aram, Dimple and I hail a cycle-rickshaw and bounce back through nighttime city streets still bustling with business. On either side of us lassi, jewellery and fabric vendors are doing a healthy trade, cycle-rickshaw bells tinkle and two-stroke delivery vans sound their horns.

'You have to think of the Aghors' sex practice through their spiritual practice,' says Aram, shouting over this audio mêlée. 'It is not about sex: it is about sex as a tool to reach the divine. So the ideal for an Aghor in his later life, like Sri

Nam, is to have used the power of sex; to have quenched himself with it and risen above it.

'In this way he is not like you and I. He is freed from the distractions of sexual pleasure. He is on his way to moksha... Remember, that's what they come to Varanasi for. The dead and the living, the city slickers, the sannyasins, they are all here for moksha.'

After I'd set out for India, Nick Black sent me an email in which he matter-of-factly described an incident from the 1970s – his years of Indian exploration – when he'd had sex with dominatrix Arione beneath a seven-tonne satanist altar complete with marble columns, statuary from various religious traditions, gargoyles, giant candelabra, lashings of black lace and broken mirrors:

> *We had sex on the floor in front of the giant altar, which inevitably lent a certain gravitas to the proceedings, and under the influence of amphetamine sulphate, which we were, leaned toward paranoid. The disadvantage of amphetamine sulphate, of course, was that you smelled like a corpse; but the advantage was that you could have sex for hours until your genitalia were blood encrusted pulp and your heart rate was around 200... Ah, good times.*

PART FOUR: THE SOUTH

Sultry down south

Silk Smitha in her prime

11 | SCREEN SIRENS, Kerala

The Indian south as celluloid fantasy fodder

The women of the Dravida country, though they are rubbed and pressed about at the time of sexual enjoyment, have a slow fall of semen; that is they are very slow in the act of coition.

—Kama Sutra, On Sexual Union, Burton translation

Dimple and I have travelled south, in second class, on the Patna–Erkalum Express, a journey that felt like enduring a 40-hour spin cycle. However, it was worth it for the pay-off of arriving in my favourite Indian state: that sliver of dense greenery sandwiched between the Arabian Sea and the Western Ghats and laced with those tourist-captivating backwaters, beautiful, bountiful Kerala.

We're here to meet a man I first encountered in 2011, when he literally crossed my path outside Mattancherry, the former Dutch colonial palace, in the Keralan city of Kochi. Chandalan Chullikkad is a poet by passion and an actor and screenplay writer for Malayalam cinema and television serials by profession. In these he often features as an avuncular figure, typically in the 2008 hit *Meena*, a soap scripted by

Chullikkad, about two warring Keralan families 'torn asunder by deceit and turmoil'. Chandy and I had swapped numbers – 'Call me Chandy!' – and in the intervening 12 months I'd received occasional, off-beat and literary text messages from him: 'I am reading some of your Shakespeare and thinking of you. Not The Taming of the Shrew, Miss Sally. Good evening. Thank you.'

I hoped Chandy would be the man to explain the sexual fixation India has on southern women. In north Indian popular culture, Kerala's women are conflated with the characteristics of its climate: sultry, tropical, fecund. They're depicted as dark and sultry, and, thanks to the genes and the strong heat of the southern Indian sun, they often are. The Indian 'whiteness' fixation has its deepest roots here, with southern Indian women spending over 30 per cent more per capita than their northern Indian counterparts on whitening products.

The Indian portrayal of the southern siren, I've often thought, recalls the British sexual stereotyping of the voluptuous southern European, their Sophia Lorens: dark and brooding, emotionally unfettered, dangerously sexy. Again, here's the use of other humans as a conduit for our sexual fantasies: the harem girls to the Victorian British males; the Sapphic eastern women to the males of the Gupta Empire; the sultry women of the Indian south to today's conservative northern Indians.

The sexual stereotyping is seen most starkly in Malayalam movies, an industry with a reputation – in India and beyond – for its sexed-up dramas, or 'soft-porn masalas', as wildly popular at home as they are in the Gulf States and among NRIs in the UK and US.

Dimple and I are investigating Kerala's export of Vaseline-lensed titillation, so now we await the actor-poet, taxi engine purring, at a villa on the outskirts of Kochi. The villa exhibits the usual hotchpotch of architectural influences: Chinese pitched roof, Islamic tiling. A jackfruit tree, auspicious to Keralan householders, stands sentinel at the entrance, and a small rubber plantation at the back of the villa grounds supplies a green-on-green horizon.

On a low concrete perimeter beside the road, a brightly painted hoarding advertises 'John O'bamas', a brand of the Western-style underpants that are gaining purchase over the traditional southern Indian cotton triangle with strings, the lunghini; and, dark red against the bright blue paint, a crudely painted hammer and sickle, electioneering for the Keralan Communist party. Nevertheless, this is not a Keralan home but a former studio where, in the heyday of Malayalam softcore, many of its biggest-grossing movies were shot.

Chullikkad arrives, pays off his taxi driver and uses the toe of his sandal to wake a guard, who's asleep, mouth agape, on a plastic garden chair by the villa entrance. We bribe him, as we had prearranged, 1000 rupees.

Inside, the windows are draped in blackout curtains made from coconut-husk hessian and it takes us a while to adjust to the gloom. We stumble into a side room to discover an old jib arm weighted by velvet layers of dust and, forlorn in the corner, a couple of reels of film. The guard trails us from room to room staring at Chandy then Dimple and I in sequence, his eyes widening as he shakes off his sleep.

We're clearly the highlight of his working year; yet it feels, I think with some disappointment, as if we've arrived long after the event, like turning up to a party when everyone's left and there's only a flat bottle of Thums Up left on the bar.

We *have* arrived late: two decades late, in fact. The peak of the Keralan softcore industry was the late 1980s. Then, strict censorship in other Indian states led Indian B-movie producers to concentrate their production in Kerala, where laws were lax and the state's actresses had grown up through the traditions of Communism and Christianity, which were – at least at that time – comparatively more permissive than states under the Hindu conservative yoke.

But it was to be a brief golden age for Kerala-produced Malayalam smut. By the late 1990s, terrorist attacks on movie studios by religious hard-liners had led to a tightening of censorship rules, and the Malayalam-language movie industry had shifted to the studios of Chennai – the capital of neighbouring Tamil Nadu – though not before Malayalam 'dirty pictures' had made their name on the world stage.

'So the south became a sexual fantasy for the north,' says Chullikkad, as we pad up the stairs and onto a landing that's littered with cigarette butts and has gaping holes that give onto the hallway below. 'We had the dark-skinned, heavy-breasted women, Dravidian women: women not civilised out of a hunger for sex.'

One of the most prolific south Indian actresses of the softcore boom years, Shakeela, has an ice cream named in her tribute in India and, in Dubai and Bahrain, two restaurants similarly christened in her honour. For the decade or so of her unchallenged reign, soft-porn movies were colloquially referred to throughout India as 'Shakeela films'. At her 2001 career peak, she appeared in a third of the 100 Malayalam-language films produced, spicing up turgid plot lines with the fluid undulations of her broad hips and 38FFs, or what she referred to, self-deprecatingly, as her 'fat, dark and buxom wares'.

Shakeela's first movie was a 1995 Tamil-language softcore outing named *Playgirls*, in which she played the sexually vampy younger sister to the most legendary of India's southern sirens, Silk Smitha.

It was to be an effective handing over of the reins as, a year later, Smitha was dead. At the age of 35, the actress-turned-producer hanged herself with an improvised noose from the ceiling fan of her Chennai apartment. She left no suicide note. The tragedy was immediately seized on by the Indian popular press, who cast her as a tragic and poignant figure.

Some argued, in sensationalist op-eds after Smitha's death, that she'd died of heartbreak; some said she feared bankruptcy after investing in a sequence of dud films; still others maintained that the traumas of her childhood had caught up with her. Whatever the truth, Smitha was immortalised as India's Marilyn Monroe, a woman, like Monroe, whose tragedy was inseparable from her sex-symbol image and hinted-at sexual transgressions.

It was an archetypical rags-to-riches story. Smitha (Sanskrit for 'divine smile') was born Vijayalakshmi Vadlapati, to an impoverished family in the southeastern state of Andra Pradesh. A poor girl from a lowly caste, married off as a child bride aged 8 and raped at 9, Vadlapati ran off in her teens to the southwest, where she found work as a touch-up artist for B-movie actresses, slept with directors to land extras parts, and was given her new name. Smitha's on-screen break came in 1979, in Malayalam movie *Inaye Thadi*, in which she played a sex worker with a heart of gold; a role that's likened to that of Julia Roberts in *Pretty Woman*. But it was 1980 Tamil-language film *Vandi Chakkram* that propelled Smitha into the big time. The role called for the then 20-year-old to jiggle her ample breasts and buttocks in a vampish dance sequence that pushed the boundaries of the censorship laws. The film was a runaway box office hit, and her character name – Silk – stuck.

She was soon typecast as a southern sexpot, commencing a prolific 16-year career that would see her dancing up to three item numbers a day for 50,000 rupees a pop. With her dusky skin and extraordinary curves, she epitomised the sexualised stereotype of the southern Indian woman and became fantasy fodder for a generation. Her fans, like enraptured sports spectators, would chant 'Silukku! Silukku!' as she danced on screen. A Smitha item could resurrect any poorly made or canned film, and many features were cobbled together off the cutting-room floor for this purpose.

'India devoured sexy Smitha,' says Chullikkad, as he finishes his telling of her tragic story. We're driving away from the abandoned studio and along a highway lined with rubber plantations and fruit trees, which are bursting forth in a compliant display of fecundity.

'But we also reviled her overt sexuality,' he continues. 'Here she was, a poor girl from rural India who'd left school aged 7; who'd been abused; whose relationships never stuck. So how could she bear such a weight of expectation?'

'Fat, dark and buxom wares' are the currency of south Indian softcore, and the broader currency of the Indian south in the north Indian imagination. It's a cliché that has its roots in Indian cultural messages about the south vs the north; Aryan vs Dravidian; white skinned vs dark skinned; safe vs sexy; and also, to an extent, in European colonial legend. Marco Polo said of his landing on the coast of Kerala: 'Men and women, they are all black, and go naked, all save a fine cloth worn about the middle'; and a seventeenth-century Dutch traveller wrote of being received by an unapologetically bare-breasted Queen of Kallada at Kerala, who was flanked by male attendants in tiny loincloths.

Of course, nakedness was far from remarkable in ancient India. Prior to the Muslim invasions, most lower-caste and tribal women went bare-breasted. In the early centuries CE there were laws prohibiting lower-caste women from covering their breasts, a privilege reserved for upper-caste females, but these depictions of open nakedness stuck to the south. They fed the stereotype of the sexy, dusky southerner that already obtained by the time of the Kamashastra.

Bare-breasted Keralan girl, 1914
(University of Southern California Digital Library)

Hindu sexology texts went to town on 'Dravidians'. Take this typical example:

> *The great duration and extreme variety of Dravidian copulation is necessitated by several anatomical peculiarities of the Dravidoid or Negroid-Australoid race. Thus, the Dravidian penis retains much of its mythical size even when flaccid, on account of its evolution as a heat exchanger to dissipate excess body heat in the warm Sudano-Deccanian climatic zone. This, coupled with the famed thickness of 'Binghi skin', implies the 'deed of kind' requires a much longer time. Moreover, Dravidian testicles, which are larger in black races, produce more sperm, requiring multiple climaxes in one night for complete release.*

In the Kama Sutra, it's a good thing Dravidian men are so equipped, as their women are 'Hastini' or 'Elephant-Women', a sexual type in possession of extremely fat buttocks and cavernous vaginas. These elephant women, the Kama Sutra asserted, would only be sated by the largest phalluses and most varied coitus; a technique referred to as 'Dravidian sex':

> *[Dravidian women are] extremely greedy for continuous congress, day and night, without food or rest. They passionately prefer the coital posture vadavahum, in which the lingam lingers for a longer period inside the yoni without emission.*

The Kama Sutra confidently continues: 'The people in the South indulge in "sex below", even in the anus.'

Darker-skinned humans are often portrayed as animalistic and sexually voracious. We saw this, of course, with the European colonial fixation on sex-hungry Orientals: the 'dark-skinned rapist', the 'lustful Indian male'. During the colonial years of the eighteenth and nineteenth centuries, the myth of the 'black super-penis' also became an obsession, perhaps fuelled by white sexual insecurity. Whatever the reason, sexual jealousy directed at a race blessed with imaginary super-penises is undoubtedly etched deep in the male psyche.

Sexual fear is certainly a catalyst for the cultural demarcation between 'black' and 'white' Indian races. Despite its palpable overtones of fear and xenophobia, I've often been struck by how large the North–South/Aryan–Dravidian divide looms in polite Indian society. I've heard it hinted at during many Delhi dinner parties, often as back-handed narcissism: 'I am so pale-skinned, when I go to the south I draw crowds'; 'Of course, the southern women are small and squat, this is why they cannot wear shalwar kameez.' Whiteness is employed to advertise fairness creams and human growth treatments; it's even used as a sales tactic for meat products – 'Buy meat and your son will grow up tall and strong, like an Aryan north Indian'.

We leave the eerie abandoned villa together to head back, with relief, to bustling Kochi. Soon the car scythes along a scenic road lined by rubber plantations. In the front seat, Chullikkad hums to the ululations of the classical Indian music cassette the driver has pushed into the dark orifice of the tape deck.

I ask Dimple if she has experienced this cultural fixation on dark Dravidian women as the eroticised competition to those who, like her, hail from the north, and have the pale complexions and height to match.

'I was aware of this fact, this difference between the north and south, quite young,' she says. 'When I was 12 my father was posted to Kerala. School in the south was a revelation. In the north I had been the wallflower: the braces-wearing girl. In the south, to my amazement, the boys thought me beautiful. I was fair, you see, compared to the southern girls. And what you have to remember is that to many Indian men, fair is beautiful. Dark has its own connotations and is something quite different. That's when I picked up the importance of being pale. That week I spent my pocket money to buy a pot of Fair & Lovely skin-whitening cream.'

'Had you known any southern women when you were in the north?' I ask her.

'Yes, we had Tamil maids for a time when I was quite young,' she says. 'They were definitely seen as, I don't know, more lowly somehow. Not beautiful. There was this sense that they weren't to be trusted. One young maid, I remember quite clearly, used to ask my mother's permission to use a little of her whitening cream. She was embarrassed by her dark skin. And I'm embarrassed when I think about all of this now. It's so accepted, but it's horrible, really, isn't it?'

We stop for a moment at a fork in the road. A Keralan woman walks in front of the car, a rubber plantation worker. She's wearing a large smile and carrying a broad-bladed coconut knife.

'And there's another thing that's happened since I was a kid,' Dimple continues. 'Whiteness has become so synonymous with beauty that even "dusky" Bollywood beauties like Priyanka Chopra endorse skin-whitening creams. I mean, goodness, Chopra is known for her dark skin. So it's like whiteness isn't even whiteness any more: it's a star quality, something impossible to see.'

There is a weak science behind the Aryan–Dravidian divide. India's original human inhabitants, the Dravidians, arrived on the subcontinent from Africa, probably on the coast at Kerala, 65,000 years ago. The gene markers of these early arrivals are still in evidence in some isolated Keralan communities. Much later, around 1500 years ago, a wave of migration from the areas that are now Eastern Europe and Turkey brought south paler-skinned people, 'Aryans', largely into the areas that are now Pakistan and the northern Indian states. However, thousands of years of intermingling of peoples on the subcontinent has put the lie to the idea of the genetic purity of any Indian caste, as shown by David Reich's 'Reconstructing Indian population history' (a 2009 paper for *Nature*).

But no matter: these days, the concepts of Aryan and Dravidian have nothing to do with genetics and everything to do with ideology. During the days of the Raj, India's highest and priestly caste, the Brahmins, co-opted Aryanism for themselves, citing their comparative whiteness as evidence of their divine right to rule. These ideas were formalised by the British, never ones to abjure the idea of white supremacy, who supported the Brahmins' claims to superiority and bestowed on them power and privileges. Through the nineteenth and twentieth centuries, Brahmin priests routinely abused these powers, claiming the right to deflower girls of lowlier castes and cherry-picking such girls to work as temple prostitutes.

We drop Chullikkad in the old spice-trading quarter of Kochi, where trade is as brisk in the aromatic hole-in-the-wall stores as it has been for ten centuries. He is planning to get stuck into some Elizabethan sonnets. Dimple and I hope to rest, and perhaps work our way through a G&T or two, before our five-hour journey back to the north of the state tomorrow. As Chullikkad bows us a polite goodbye, I ask him what his take is on these time-worn polarities of north–south and white–dark.

'It's about mythology,' he says, after a moment's thought, 'a mythology that's grown up around the early settlers in the south, and the later Aryan invaders in the north. It's about the story that India tells herself, about herself. You have to understand that in India we had no age of reason, as you did in the West. So instead of the process of logic, we have mythology. That's why Marxism became such a weird and wonderful hybrid on Keralan soil.'

I murmur in agreement. Only in India can a 'communist' run for local election on the promise of encouraging inward investment from Western multinationals.

'And why your sexual revolution will be so different from ours in the West?' I add, picking up a conversation we'd stared earlier, as he'd run us through Silk Smitha's titillating oeuvre.

'Yes,' says Chullikkad. 'For you it was about science, about cause and effect, the arrival of the contraceptive pill and what came next. For us in India it's about mythology, about finding Tantrism again, about rediscovering the great Indian love stories and reclaiming our spiritual right.'

12 | DIRTY DANCING, Kerala

The erotic dance tradition banned by the Raj, now resurgent with young Indians

A female, therefore, should learn the Kama Shastra, or at least a part of it, by studying its practice from some confidential friend. She should study alone in private the sixty-four practices that form a part of the Kama Shastra. The following are the arts to be studied, together with the Kama Sutra: Singing, Playing on musical instruments, Dancing, Union of dancing, singing, and playing instrumental music.

—Kama Sutra, Book One, General Observations, Doniger/Kakar translation, 2002

'Victorian Britishers have a lot to answer for, Miss Sally and Miss Dimple... Yes.'

It's a complaint Dimple and I have heard variously during our journey across the east and north of the subcontinent. Our current complainant, Kaladharan Viswanath, has perhaps less cause for hard feelings than many who've advanced the same opinion. He is head of Kalamandalam, a Keralan dance school founded in the 1930s that's suddenly booming, with an oversubscription of young Indians vying for a place on its full-time seven-year courses.

Dimple and I are suffering stinging eyes and heavy heads. It's the morning after our trip to the abandoned studio and we'd stayed up until 3 a.m., sloshing the gin we'd smuggled into what – we'd been dismayed to discover – was a dry, all-veg ayurvedic hotel.

Now we're queasily embarking on a bumpy four-hour journey with Viswanath to Kalamandalam, based in the Keralan cultural capital at Thrissur. An hour in and the scenery is helping a little to soothe my throbbing brow: locals smile from roadside toddy stalls; ostentatious mansions, built with the wealth sent back by the 30 per cent of young Keralans who head to the Gulf to work in construction and nursing, peek out from between rubber plantations and coconut palms.

Kalamandalam is named for Kalamandalam Kalyanikutty Amma, a Mohinyattam dancer who braved 1930s societal disapproval and the censure of the Raj to resurrect the sultry dance tradition, founding the school's Mohiniyattam department.

'Victorian morality planted in Indian soil with theological force,' Viswanath continues, 'and there were many, many victims. Hijras and tawaifs [concubines] lost their courtly patronage, and many music and dance traditions associated with these groups suffered. Mohiniyattam, for example, was depicted as a dance of the temple prostitutes, the devadasis – inaccurately, of course.'

Believed to have originated in the sixteenth century, Mohiniyattam is one of the eight classical dance forms recognised by the Indian government national academy for the performing arts, Sangeet Natak Akademi. Kathakali, the second of the great eight to hail from Kerala, is distinguished by its dramatic plot lines, expressive gestures and

Mohiniyattam dancers

bright face-painting, and is principally a male dance tradition. In contrast, Mohiniyattam centres round solo recitals by female performers.

The intention of the dance is to conjure sringara rasa, one of the nine rasas, or emotional sentiments, that Indian artistic traditions aim to evoke (from hāsyam, or mirth, to kāruyam, tragedy, and vīram, or heroic mood). An emotional theme with no direct English translation, sringara is often described as something between erotic love and beauty. Of the nine rasas, sringara rasa is known as the king of sentiments (rajarasa). The invocation of sringara rasa in Indian art ranges from the grotesque, as seen in the grand gestures of fear and anger in the Keralan theatre tradition of Koodiyattam, to a refined or subtle take on the mood, like in the fluid Tamil Nadan classical dance from Bharathanatyam, or the flowing dance of

Mohiniyattam. Locally, Mohiniyattam's sinuous movements are likened to Kerala's swaying palms.

'The tradition was eventually banned by the British really quite surprisingly late, in 1925 – though the seeds of its demise were sown with the crackdowns after the rebellion of 1857,' Viswanath explains.

Now Mohiniyattam is being reclaimed as a historical Indian art, as a celebration of femininity, he explains as we restore ourselves after the journey with idli rice dumplings and coconut chutney at a café near the school. Yet, like the devadasi tradition, we are warned to be careful in describing this as anything to do with female empowerment.

'Mohiniyattam promotes a male-centric vision of how women should be,' he says. 'You know, coy, pliant, coaxing; suffering intolerable angst when separated from their powerful lover, a figure who's a proxy for a deity, love and feudal lord. So it's complex adapting these ideas for the modern time. But it should be seen through the sixteenth-century world in which the tradition came about. This was an India of powerful male groups, in which lower castes were largely playthings of the Brahmins. Mohiniyattam is a postcard, a very pretty one, from a bygone age.'

The development of Mohiniyattam coincided with the westerly push of the Telugu Brahmins into Kerala, Viswanath explains as we order another platter of idli.

'The Brahmins arrived, and they created a sensation. They were intellectually advanced. They could calculate time and predict the coming week's weather, skills which were understood by the Keralans to be godly,' he continues.

Like eighteenth-century European girls schooled in feminine accomplishments, or surgically enhanced would-be footballers' wives in modern-day Britain, young women saw mastery of the feminine art form of Mohiniyattam as a means to the end of securing a coveted association with a powerful man.

'There was a wilful surrender to the desires and fancies of the Brahmins,' he says. 'For women it was seen as a heavenly blessing to bear a Brahmin child.'

Viswanath darts off to his office and Dimple and I tag along with a group of American visitors on a tour of the Kalamandalam campus. Thrissur is inland, far from the cooling Arabian sea breezes, and the mercury's already inching into the 40s. The heat has parched the clay soil a stark red-yellow and made the leaves of the neem and peeple trees curl up in protest.

It's spring, so soon the monsoon will break, bringing with it the three months of downpours responsible for the annual greening of the garden state. For now, the Kalamandalam students are beaded with sweat, into their third hour of morning tuition in the traditional windowless stone classrooms that dot the campus grounds. In one classroom 10- and 11-year-old boys, bare breasted and dressed in the simple southern Indian sarong, the lunghi, bang out complex rhythms on rustic-looking drums.

'That's the Madhalam,' says Latika, an administrator for Kalamandalam who's leading the site tour. 'It's a traditional drum made out of the jackfruit tree that's important in Kathakali accompaniment.'

We pass a classroom where Kathakali dancers practise: standing in one-legged, bent-kneed poses, contorting their eyebrows into the exaggerated, almost campy depictions of emotion typical of the art. We walk on, to a classroom deeper into the campus grounds, passing the make-up room, where all of the artistic tools of Keralan dance are housed: pigments and charcoals and the chundanga seeds dancers insert near to their tear ducts, to give their eyes a bloodshot appearance.

At the next classroom, I find what I've been looking for: a group of 20 young women practising Mohiniyattam. They're not yet wearing their heavy eye make-up and white-and-gold costumes of the Mohini – the dhoti with jarikar border worn around abdomen and chest, the hair bunched on the side of the head and dressed with a white flower – but still, their moves are unmistakable: posture erect, their hips swaying from side to side in gentle, sinuous motion.

The girls' mobile eyes hint one minute of modesty, the next surprise, then coquetry; their hands articulate the distinctive sign language of Mohiniyattam – now the cupped palms, fingers splayed, of the lotus-flower position; now the pinched index finger and thumb and arched ring finger of the peacock pose.

Latika approaches as we watch, whispering an explanation. 'This is Aliveni Enthu Chevyu. It's one of the padams, or love songs, of Mohiniyattam. It was composed by Maharaja Swathi Thirunal, a nineteenth-century king who was an important patron and practitioner of the dance form.'

I ask what the narrative is.

'The heroine is talking to her dear friend who is endowed with long, beautiful curly hair,' says Latika. 'She addresses her friend as "Aliveni", which means "one who resembles a beehive", and says: "What am I to do, for my lotus-eyed lover has not come to me yet? The moonlit night, the cooing of the cuckoos, the sweet scented flowers and the variety of flowers, of what use is this, if my beloved does not come to me?"'

In this plaintive lament, the Mohiniyattam dancer of Aliveni Enthu Chevyu is characteristic of Virahotkhandita Nayika, one of eight types of heroines delineated in the Natya Shastra, an ancient Indian treatise on the performing arts (written around 200 BCE). It's said to be the embodiment of female romantic longing. She is not able to bear the pangs of separation from her lover and yearns to be reunited with him.

In the rough and tumble of sexed-up, sexually repressed modern India, romantic stories such as this are often lost: Shah Jahan and Mumtaz Mahal (of the Taj Mahal); or Rama gathering an army of monkeys to search for an exiled Sita (if you forget that Sita walked through fire to prove her chastity, inspiring many thousands of copycat immolations). So I can see the appeal of the extreme emotions invested in these narratives. Stories such as that of bold Natya Shastra, a ballsy heroine who braves storms, thunder and snakes in a fevered midnight pursuit of her lover, are surely more appealing than the drab present-day Indian adaptation of love to duty in the love-cum-arranged marriage.

Dimple and I join the Mohinis' line and try to copy their fluid movements. A foot taller than most of the girls, I'm nothing less than conspicuous.

'You look a little like a tree blowing in the monsoon, Sally,' laughs Dimple. Twenty girls giggle uproariously.

Dimple fares better, though at 5 ft 4 in, it's easier for her to undulate on command.

As the class trails out for lunch, Dimple and I meet a couple of girls for a chat in a resinous wood-panelled library. Reshma Gopinath is 23 years old and resembles a south Indian Vanessa Paradis, with a catlike face and large, limpid eyes.

'I chose Mohiniyattam as a means of self-expression,' she says, 'I express my own emotions through the heroines. I identify with their anguish and lamentation.'

Seethu Mohan, also 23, nods vigorously in agreement, her pigtails bouncing up and down like restless snakes. 'What's difficult in Mohiniyattam is the sringara. It's an emotion that's difficult to express until you have experience in life, and love. I have no experience with sex and love, so in a way I improvise,' she tells us.

'How do you improvise?' Dimple asks.

Mohan colours at this, and gazes out of the window at the intense sun. 'I suppose I think what it would be like to have a boyfriend; though I have never had a boyfriend.

'But,' she adds shyly, after a pause, 'when I do get a boyfriend I will know what to do... I am growing up as a woman through the dance of Mohiniyattam.'

The girls' naivety is at odds with the British depiction of 'Oriental' dancers as brazen and sexually overt. In the nineteenth century, as with the Middle Eastern tradition of belly-dance or raqs sharqi (which was in fact often performed by women for women, as an act of sisterly bonding and self-expression), the lines between Indian female dance forms and prostitution were hopelessly blurred. Nowhere was this more seen than in the tradition of courtly dance, or mujra.

The sensual dance of the tawaifs, mujra dates back to the Mughal Empire of the sixteenth to eighteenth centuries, a period during which there was an explosion of art forms in the Indus Valley. But from the 1800s, tawaifs became a key focus of the Raj's moral crackdown. There were political reasons for this, too: mujra performances had provided an opportunity for mutineers to meet and many tawaifs were actively involved in the movement. The British confiscated many of the tawaif kothas (houses) after the mutiny, disrupting tawaif teaching and succession.

So by the early 1900s, many tawaifs had moved into prostitution. But like many of these ancient Indian traditions, their community endured. Some tawaifs went into early Bollywood, with mujra dancing items becoming a staple of Hindi films in the 1960s and 1970s. Others even recalcitrantly clung to their old patronage. It's said that when attempts were made to convert the Lake Palace at Udaipur into a luxury hotel in the 1960s, the then regent, Bhagwat Singh, encountered stiff resistance from the palace's tawaifs-in-residence.

In the account of Didi Contractor, an American design consultant on the Udaipur job:

> *When he came to the throne he inherited big problems, like what to do with the 300 dancing girls that belonged to his predecessor [Maharana Bhopal Singh]. He tried to offer them scholarships to become nurses but they didn't want to move out of the palace, so what could he do? He had to keep them. They were old crones by this time and on state occasions I remember they would come to sing and dance with their ghunghats [veils] down and occasionally one would lift hers to show a wizened old face underneath. And he also had something like twelve state elephants.*

On another site, a ten-minute drive from Kalamandalam, we catch up with Leela Mar, one of the school's heads and a Mohiniyattam dancer for 50 years. She has the perfect posture and neat hairdo of a superannuated ballet dancer.

'The girls were correct,' she says. 'Mohiniyattam is, above all, about the play of womanhood. It's an expressional form of dance, in which your whole body reacts.

'So not all girls are suitable for Mohiniyattam. Many don't have the temperament to dance Mohiniyattam, as it's both mental and physical. So we test them for their aptitude as young girls. But if you really live the dance, it can be your salvation; especially in our difficult modern society.'

This is an idea we pick up with Viswanath when we seek him out a few hours later. He's looking fatigued by the moist heat and, I suspect, by the sheer piles of international correspondence piled up on his desk – testament to the interest the wider dancing world is beginning to show in Kalamandalam.

And it's not only dance enthusiasts abroad who are bombarding Viswanath. India's middle classes are also focusing their attentions, and burgeoning spending power, on the old Indian art forms: they're collecting fine-art textiles, they're supporting Sufi musicians and they're patronising Indian dance. Mujra dancing has become a faddish addition to wedding entertainment for the well-to-do and Viswanath's brightest graduates land gigs in cities across the subcontinent.

'There are good and bad things about our modern times,' he says, his forehead beading with sweat in the sticky heat. 'There is more money in India, so now these young artists you see around you have a real hope of an income from their craft. They will dance at shows and at private parties thrown for the rich of shining India. But at the same time, attention spans are getting shorter. The grand narratives of dance are being lost.

'Modern life, as I see it, is all about an enactment of emotion rather than the feeling of emotion. So I work hard with the kids here to nurture their wild flames of passion. This, as I see it, is my vocation. But it's a difficult thing: wild flames of passion and cell phones do not easily exist in the same life,' he concludes.

It's the end of the school day and students are milling around campus: giggling thickets of girls, boys running through their dance positionings on patches of sun-scorched grass.

Dimple and I find our cab driver and splay ourselves across the back seat for the long journey south, back to Kochi. Drowsily, we chat about what we've seen in Kerala.

'You know, Kerala does have this mystical thing,' says Dimple, 'this land of plantations and smiles. So I understand why it's romanticised by northern Indians.'

'And by American retirees, too,' I say. 'Is that why they come, do you think?'

'They come for the reason you've come, gori,' says Dimple. 'They come because your countries are monochrome. But here in southern India, India is in Technicolor: Technicolor in life; Technicolor in love.'

She's right. The reason India is so instructive in these matters of love and life is because it's all here. Even in a modern India fixated on the twenty-first-century dream, the India of the Tantras, the Kama Sutra and the Raj lives on, with all of its concomitant and conflicting takes on love, sex and sexuality. Unlike in the West – where we arrogantly assume we're living a life that's the summation of all human knowledge – here there is no one truth. That is why India is so illuminating and, of course, so bloody infuriating.

I wonder what's left to come, smiling across at the now snoozing Dimple, as I settle myself down for a bumpy ride.

13 | CALLING DR LOVE, Chennai

Sex doctor tourism in the city of fire

A man who understands the heart should
enlarge his repertory of techniques for sexual ecstasy
by this means and that, imitating the amorous
movements
of tame animals, wild animals, and birds.
When these various moods are evoked
According to the particular nature of the woman
And of her region, they inspire
Women's affection, passion and respect.

—Kama Sutra, Book Two, On Sexual Union,
Doniger/Kakar translation, 2002

Listening to my moans as you touch certain spots,
The parrot mimics me, and O how we laugh in bed!
You say, 'Come close, my girl'
And make love to me like a wild man, Muvva Gopla,
And as I get ready to move on top,
It's morning already!

—Kshetrayya, itinerant Telagu poet, seventeenth century

The electricity has outed for the third time in less than an hour. Dr Reddy tugs the pull-cord on his Roman blind and throws open the window of his Chennai office. Outside, rickshaw and moped horns bleat helplessly as vehicles concertina at a failed traffic light.

'I'm sorry, I'm sorry girls – ladies. Here you see our tragic flaw of Chennai!'

Rolling blackouts and load shedding owing to electricity undersupply benight modern India, though with daily power outages, Chennai is currently the worst affected of the major Indian cities. It's in the summer months, when the mercury creeps up to the early 40s °C and even Chennaiites are reliably decorated with rivulets of perspiration, that citizens bemoan the nickname of the 'city of fire'.

For now, Dr Narayana Reddy, Chennai's premier sexologist, suffers the blackouts several times a day with practised sangfroid.

'Tell me, what can you do? What can you do? The five-star hotels have their power, and the politicians' district. The rest of us? Hospital patients? Hah!' he tells us.

In the northeast corner of the state of Tamil Nadu – home to Tamil, the world last surviving classical civilisation and last living classical language – sits Chennai, India's fourth largest city. Giving out to the sheening vastness of the Bay of Bengal, Chennai is hot, fast and congested. As a major transport hub, many tourists pass through the Tamil capital en route to the more crowd-pleasing outposts of the south; however, others stick around for the culture. This is not surprising, perhaps, as Chennai is renowned for its south Indian classical music and dance traditions, showcased annually at Masam Marghazi, an arts festival that has blossomed into one of the largest cultural events in the world, attracting, in the 2012–13 season, over a million out-of-town visitors to 1200 events.

To some, Chennai is seen as a conservative city: the lunghi and business shirt look is big here; neighbourhoods in the original city are still divided along caste lines; and traders in Georgetown congregate in streets according to what they sell. Yet Tamil Nadu also lives comfortably in modernity. Chennai is the location of one of India's few women-only police stations. It's where Bharathi, India's first transgender pastor, preaches to an appreciative crowd. It's also the only one of India's four major cities with room to expand; and it's doing so, with alacrity. Dimple and I had taken a tour of the new Chennai the morning we arrived, all shiny twenty-first-century property developments pushing along the coastline of the Bay of Bengal.

Chennai is home, too, to what Dimple and I have chiefly come here to see: a thriving industry of destination sexology clinics. The sex clinics attract visiting Indians – some candid metropolitan couples, many sheepish newlyweds – from across the subcontinent. Some clients come in response to spam SMS sent to cellphones: 'Sad wife? Ayurveda prolong her satisfaction'. Some respond to adverts in the national press; still others follow the fame of specialists such as Dr Reddy.

He charges 1000 rupees (about £11) for a first consultation in his three by three metre office in T Nagar, south-central Chennai. He's one of this new discipline's most illustrious practitioners. Reddy chose the specialism after graduating in general medicine in the early 1980s. Back then he was ahead of his time.

'My fellow medical students thought I was raving mad,' he tells us, his eyes twinkling with implied self-congratulation. 'They chose specialisms in heart and eye surgery. And they laughed at me. "Who will come to consult you?" they said. You see, there was a big stigma back then about admitting to sexual dysfunction. There's still a stigma now, of course. But the people came; although it took me until the twenty-first century to find a woman who was willing to work as my secretary!'

It all changed, he tells us, in 1985 with the first Indian general synod on sexuality. 'It was the time when HIV was beginning to rampage here. The world's media came. At last the Indian medical profession began to talk about this area; this area that's so much part of human life.'

Things have changed drastically since the late 1990s, continues Reddy, after apologising for offering us no chai due to the power outage. The turning point, he says, was 1997. 'That was the very year the Indian media got wind of the fact that sex sells. I began to write a sex advice column for a Chennai magazine, and the magazine's circulation quadrupled to 150,000. Now I write sex columns that syndicate across 19 titles, all through India.'

I nod. The Indian tabloid pink press always had its share of scantily clad wannabe actresses. But in my more recent trips to the subcontinent, there seemed to have been a mood shift. Today, Indian publishing's love affair with sex screams out from every racy strap-line or gratuitous excuse to focus on sex scandals in parliament, or the reproachable habits of India's youth. Nevertheless, as I'd seen when I met *Cosmopolitan India* editor Nandini Bhalla, these magazines tread a tightrope: reflecting the mores of a nominally conservative nation while simultaneously sating its irrepressible appetite for all things sex.

As far as Reddy's concerned, the trend for all these column inches treating of (ostensibly conjugal) pleasures is far from simply rank titillation and magazine sales. In a nation where no or patchy sex education is the norm, his articles provide a public service. Reddy's recent syndicated columns – and where I'd first discovered him, when idly flicking through a newspaper on the *Delhi Metro* – have included: 'Is it the woman's fault if she cannot produce a boy?' and 'Are my nocturnal emissions making me ill?'

'My columns are read by workers,' he says, 'by bus and autorickshaw drivers; by wives who pick up a second-hand magazine when they're out shopping for veg in the local market. For many, this is the first – and only – sexual education they will have. Still today, many couples come to me absolutely ignorant. They have no idea how to conceive.'

This reminds me of an illuminating conversation I had a few years ago with an elderly medic. The doctor, whom I met at a London wedding, had worked as a general practitioner in a Catholic village in Ireland during the 1950s and 1960s. Over wedding-reception Prosecco, he told me that on two occasions during his years as a GP, young wives unable to conceive had presented to him bearing bruises around their belly buttons. It's here, in the umbilicus, that their husbands had been endeavouring to insert their respective penises.

But ignorance, for young Irish and Indian couples alike, is far from bliss. Dr Reddy taps the cover of a book on the desk in front of him, one of his own. Three copies are fanned out in the kind of display you might see in the dinner-party napkins of a 1950s American housewife. The cover reads *Making Sense*, the subtitle *A Handbook for the To-Be Married*.

'I find young Indian couples need the very basics,' he says. 'They can have no hope of a happy sex life until I impart the basic teaching that Indian society has denied them.'

The lot of many young Indians, I think to myself, must be similar to that of Victorian British women kept intentionally innocent. Or the fate of the many ignorant wedding-night wives frigid due to sheer fear. Or, as Kama Sutra translator Richard Burton put it in his discussion of the superior pleasures to be found in the arms of 'Oriental' women, British women were schooled into sexual over-delicacy, to 'porcelain where pottery is wanted'.

Dr Reddy and the new media-friendly Indian sexologists are performing a function similar to that of Dr Marie Stopes. Her trailblazing *Married Love, or Love in Marriage* was first published in England in 1918. The book, which talked in unfussy terms about the techniques and functions of sex, was banned as obscene on its release in Edwardian England; though it eventually brought about a quiet revolution, propelled by broader social changes, in Britain's discourse around sex.

Dimple, who's been listening quietly to Reddy's state-of-the-nation sex report, suddenly pipes up, '*Baywatch*!'

'What?' I ask, startled from my reverie, and wondering whether her blood-sugar levels have crashed. Since our arrival at Chennai she's been gorging on doodh peda, the city's famous milk fudge. Grand Sweets in Adyar, where the most famous versions of these ear-tingly sweet sweets are sold, was our first port of call in Chennai, straight off the Guwahati Express from Ernakulum Junction; an overnight express train that was stocked with rabid mosquitoes and neatly moustached regional politicians. Since our arrival, Dimple has masticated as ferociously as I have scratched.

'That's where my former husband learned sex: *Baywatch*,' she elaborates, addressing Dr Reddy. 'This was before porn arrived on every Indian handphone. So it was from *Baywatch*. And from Bollywood movies of the 1980s, where the woman's breasts heave up and down and she looks coy and prances about beneath a waterfall, or a bad guy moves in on her, and he's frothing like a rabies case, and she's whispering 'Main vaisi ki ladki nahin hoon' [I'm not that kind of girl].'

Baywatch. Many Indian 20- and 30-something males nurture fond memories of the pneumatic 1980s lifeguard drama, which continues to run to healthy viewing figures on the Starworld India television channel. Likewise, British comedy series *The Benny Hill Show*, in which the eponymous star chases bikini-clad women about the British countryside, is often on high-speed playback. It ran for seven seasons on India's UTV and was dubbed into nine Indian languages.

Dimple warms to her theme as the electricity sputters to life. The ceiling fan above us stirs one full 360 then shudders off again.

'You know, the consummation of my marriage was like being kicked, or hit with a cricket bat,' she says. 'I was just prodded: prodded with a penis, in silence. No love. But how could there be love? Arranged marriage: love-shove.'

I'm surprised. Dr Reddy must inspire confidences. I'd tried and failed to learn about Dimple's marital sex life before. Like many Westerners, I've always been intrigued by what comes next in an arranged marriage, after the ceremonials. I've struggled as I tried to imagine myself in the position of being expected to perform, sexually, with a virtual stranger.

The Kama Sutra advises how a good citizen, having chosen his virginal bride (taking care to check his carrion for bad omens such as sweating palms, blemishes and 'crooked thighs'), might seduce her three days after their wedding night. After a couple of days' bathing, decorating themselves and 'listening to auspicious instruments', says Vatsyayana:

> *The man should begin to win her over and create confidence in her, but should abstain at first from sexual pleasures. Women being of tender nature want tender beginnings, and when they are forcibly approached by men with whom they are but slightly acquainted, they sometimes suddenly become haters of sexual connection, and sometimes even haters of the male sex.*

I also found striking Indian journalist Khushwant Singh's account of being an unwilling observer to consummation of an arranged marriage on the night train from Delhi to Bhopal:

> *The saree is very functional. All a woman has to do when she wants to urinate or defecate is to lift it to her waist. When required to engage in sexual intercourse, she needs to do no more than draw it up a little and open her thighs... Apparently this was what the newly married Mrs Saxena was called upon to do. I heard a muffled cry 'Hai Ram' escape her lips and realized that the marriage had been consummated. The Saxenas did not get up to go to the bathroom to wash themselves but began a repeat performance. More than once the quilt slipped and I caught a glimpse of the professor's heaving buttocks and his bride's bosom, which he had extricated out of her choli. Above the rattle and whish of the speeding train I heard the girl's whimper and the man's exulting grunts. In the morning, when I pressed the switch in the compartment – a memorable sight! Professor fast asleep with his buttocks exposed. Mrs Saxena also fast asleep, her mouth wide, breasts bare, lying supine like a battery pinned down on a board. Their glasses lay on the floor.*

Even if they overcome the grim fact of being strangers to one another, for many lower- and middling-caste Indian newly-weds the concept of privacy is as alien as that of love.

I once saw the typical experience described as follows. The young married couple will rarely get a room to themselves, the bride-wife sleeping with the other women members of her husband's family and the husband lining up his charpoy (woven daybed) alongside his brother's and father's. Occasionally the mother-in-law, anxious to gain a grandson, will contrive a meeting between the husband and his wife by, perhaps, getting her to take him a tumbler of milk, whereupon her son will be expected to grab the chance for a quickie. Rarely will the couple get the opportunity for a prolonged and satisfying bout of intercourse.

Understandably, many young married Indian men are unaware that women have orgasms; and many Indian women rebound from one pregnancy to the next with no idea that sex can be pleasurable.

Even if the young couple overcomes the twin disablements of having married a stranger and finding a private space to themselves, it's likely there will be an elephant in that room. Or rather, a sprawling extended family.

'In the West a man marries the woman and the woman marries a man,' Reddy continues, when I ask him how his clients cope with the brute facts of arranged married life in twenty-first-century India, 'whereas in India we marry our family-in-law too. And the marriage is a contract between two families. So if my son malfunctions sexually, his wife's family will blame me.

'For most families the sole intention of the marriage is issue. If the woman does not get pregnant two or three months after the wedding they start to worry. "Any good news?" they will say, "Any good news?" How do you think that affects a young couple's sex life? What should be a story about when you're in the mood becomes an act in obligation to your parents-in-law. And I know you girls can't quite put yourselves in that position,' Reddy says, smiling. 'But that would give me erectile dysfunction...

'There's one remarkable thing I'm seeing,' he continues as he fiddles with his blind to achieve a little daylight in the gloomy room. 'Thanks to all the money of "India rising" something quite peculiar is going on. Cases are coming to me where parents are litigating in complaint that their daughter has been married off to a sexually deficient spouse.'

'God, what does that mean?' I ask.

'I'll tell you how it typically goes,' says Reddy. 'The couple is married, but no child has come. It's because the boy can't perform and she tells her parents this.

'Now, a few years ago, the girl would be blamed. Instead, today, the family sees dollar signs. They take the case to family court to get a separation, putting forward the argument that the boy is "faulty goods". Then, the boy might be arrested. There could be criminal proceedings. If the boy's declared a cheater, or gay, or proved to be in love with a girl from another caste, they might get higher compensation.'

Dimple's eyes widen. Reddy notes her reaction.

'I know.... a few years ago, I would have thought this situation remarkable; today it happens time and again. And the sad truth is that many of the boys in these situations will actually be gay,' he says, shaking his head bleakly, as he echoes what Mavendra Singh Gohil told us back in Rajpipla. 'But marriage is still seen as the great cure in India. So your son says he's gay? OK, maybe you think he's gay, but you'll marry him off anyway. Marriage will cure him! If he's mentally ill, marriage will cure him! Just don't tell his wife or her family; they don't have to know: just a phase, auntie, just a phase!

'Because you see,' Reddy says, after a stagey pause, 'for Indians, marriage must take place at any cost: "Even if you have to tell tell 100 lies", the saying goes, "get the couple married".'

I ask him how he treats such sexually doomed unions, in a land where divorce is still comparatively rare.

'Of course, I cannot say "You two will never get along, you must separate". Right or wrong, the pressure for everyone will be to hold on to a marriage; they will have come to me, often, with their family members, who are also invested in their marriage. I tread a careful line.

'That said, India is in a transition phase,' he continues. 'These attitudes have receded from the Westernised upper-middle classes. The same, I hope, will happen in other areas.'

For now, Reddy focuses on talking therapies, he tells us, gingerly navigating his way through the quagmire of societal pressures. 'So the men come to me concerned about whether they can rise to the occasion, or not,' he explains. 'That is all that they worry about. They don't look at emotion, though they should. Women come to me worried about the fact men cannot understand their feelings. I have what I call a Shakti Clinic for women's marital issues.'

It's a funny setting in which to hear the word Shakti, or primordial female creative power, once again. In this usage it corroborates what Chullikkad told us: that India's will be a sexual revolution with spiritual characteristics. Or perhaps, in another interpretation, that old Hindu ideas are being deployed for a new purpose: to sweeten, or 'Indianise', the nation's breakneck pace of change.

I ask Reddy about ayurvedic sexology. Since my arrival in India I'd seen numerous advertisements offering sexual satisfaction via ayurveda. I'd even received text messages to my mobile phone offering 'erections guaranteed. Phone this number, expert in Ayurveda'.

Reddy rolls his eyes at this. 'These people have the best intentions; and the better clinics can certainly help with the Western problem of mind and body separation, and perhaps sexual dysfunctions.

'The problem is that ayurveda in the field of sexology is largely quackery in India today. There are many people who trade on fear and ignorance. There are quack ayurveda practioners who advertise on Hindi music channels after 11.30

with some second-grade Bollywood actor endorsing their products.'

'What do they sell?' I ask him.

'Well, I certainly would not consume it,' he replies. 'They mix all sorts of powders into their ayurvedic cures, including heavy metal compounds such as mercury. If you're lucky you'll get a small amount of a generic Viagra; and they give Viagra and mercury mixes to women for fertility too, of course. Viagra is the great cure-all. I wish people would take these ayurvedic sexologists with a bag of salt. But this is incredible, credulous India. And they don't.'

Such quakery and obfuscation are in marked contrast to the sex education regimen proposed by the Kama Sutra. Young men and woman alike, contends Vatsyayana:

> *should study the Kama Sutra and the arts and sciences subordinate thereto, in addition to the study of the arts and sciences contained in the Dharma and Artha. Even young maids should study the Kama Sutra with its arts and sciences before marriage.*

There's a tap on the door, which creaks open to display the head and shoulders of a middle-aged woman. She's wearing a classy silk saree and neat spectacles, above which her forehead tilak is smudged. It makes her look, endearingly, like a librarian who's mistakenly classified herself for the bookshelf.

'Madams, I have a client waiting,' says Reddy, addressing us. 'So! What do I tell you before you leave?'

I'm unsure whether or not this is intended as a rhetorical question. Dimple and I glance at one another.

'I will tell you,' Reddy says, rubbing his hands together, and speaking rather grandly, 'my predictions for what comes next...

'There is a lot of change in India.... a lot of change. You see it in Bollywood. There's no strings-attached-sex in romantic comedy, a new romantic narrative of the love union: big hits like *Hum Tum Bihag Bhatt* [My Brother's Fiancée] and *Rockstar*, where premarital sex is shown. Of course, at the end of movies they'll live together like goody-goody people. Still, the message is revolutionary. The message is this: we're doing it, and we're not feeling bad about it.

'I see the same in the letters I receive, too. These days the women say: "Yes, I am doing it." Don't mistake that this is a huge change. The problem is,' Reddy says, pointing at each of us in turn. 'You two….'

'Is it?' says Dimple.

'Yes,' he asserts, 'you two; or, rather, the fact that the Indian man cannot reconcile the two of you. He cannot cope with the Westernised Indian woman.

'Naturally he likes the idea, with his hands between his legs, in bed at night. But at the end of the day, he wants to marry his mother; he wants a Good Indian Girl. The Indian male is 10, maybe 15 years behind the Indian woman.'

Dimple and I walk through the dark reception past a group of adults. Three middle-aged women talk gregariously, sharing a paper bag of green sweets. At their centre, side by side, sit a young man and woman, in silence.

As we pass them, I wonder if they know there's a revolution afoot.

14 | BOLLYWOOD CONFIDENTIAL, Bombay

Bar girls and the flesh trade

I now commenced a regular course of fucking with native women. They understand in perfection all the arts and wiles of love, are capable of gratifying any tastes, and in face and figure they are unsurpassed by any women in the world... It is impossible to describe the enjoyment I experienced in the arms of these syrens. I have had English, French, German and Polish women of all grades of society since, but never, never did they bear a comparison with those salacious, succulent houris of the East.

—*Captain Edward Sellon (1818–66)*

We've crossed the tip of India to the other, western coast, to the state of Maharastra, home to India's rich agricultural hinterland of Pune, where Osho's lavish commune lives on, and to India's most vibrant city and commercial capital, Bombay.

Dimple and I arrive in the city one impossibly hot late spring morning, in a vile mood, having been held captive on searing hot tarmac for two hours by the faulty electrics of our Kingfisher Airlines aircraft. Early during this ordeal, an elderly Gujarati woman had hyperventilated, and the air hostesses and pilot had screamed at mutinying passengers to sit down. Ninety minutes into the ordeal piped background music, the only electrical function still apparently operating on our ailing Airbus, struck up with Phil Collins' 'Another Day in Paradise'. With unhinged hilarity, the cabin had erupted into laughter.

A few days later, we'd learn that the airline's staff hadn't been paid for a month, and the airline itself, run by notorious Indian beer magnate and playboy Vijay Mallya, had pulled half its routes and was on the brink of receivership.

Eventually we decant onto blistering tarmac and make it through an arrivals hall thronged with extended families awaiting relatives in festive mood, and cab drivers touting for trade. Presently, an airport porter demands 50 rupees to carry our suitcases three metres to the taxi stand. We get in the taxi, an AC-fitted Kool Cab we've paid over the odds for but whose aircon unit is kaput, and a young man on a motorbike hands me a note of his phone number through the open window. He makes the international hand sign for 'give me a call', winks at Dimple, then weaves off into the traffic.

'Welcome to Bombay,' Dimple smiles.

Landing in Bombay – or Mumbai as its official name became in 1995, but which only journalists and careful foreigners call it – always feels a little like arriving in New York: an onslaught of antagonistic taxi drivers, and people screaming at each other in the streets in tones reserved in Britain for begging for a near-relative's life. Or perhaps how it might have been to arrive in Victorian London, as breathlessly vital and as vile as anything Charles Dickens could imagine.

From its Bollywood strugglers to its Indian Premier League cricket wannabes (drawn by the promise of IPL's mega pay packets), this is the city where everyone, in the words of an Indian billboard ad, wants to go 'from zero to hero'. Bombay is modern India's great shopfront. Whether it's power, prostitution or dinner you're after, this is where it's at.

It's also, with stiff competition, my favourite Indian city. I love the fact that it's a place taking flight, throbbing with the energy and ambition of its 14 million inhabitants and the tens of thousands of souls who arrive here each month hoping to make good their dreams. Many of these new arrivals end up in Dharavi, Asia's largest slum, where one million poor squat some of the world's most sought-after real estate, sharing one toilet to 1440 digestive tracts.

Dimple and I are the lucky ones. We're bound not for the slums or the tourist-clogged south of Bombay, but for the very heights of 'hi-fi' Bombay: Juhu, our base for a month, and the city's most affluent suburb.

Our home is a three-bedroom duplex, where we eventually arrive after tortuously charting every back street of the western suburbs. Our taxi driver had employed the navigation tactic of all Bombay cab drivers, always infuriating, of stopping at every intersection to ask directions of the nearest person, only to hare off every five minutes or so in contrary directions.

Our apartment features all the staples demanded of a Bombay des-res: uniformed and armed security guards; morning delivery of everything from newspapers to tender green drinking coconuts; small child servants sleeping in the stairwell among the rats churned up by the unceasing construction work. It also features our roommate, Sanvi. At 1 p.m. we find her lounging on her apartment sofa in a silk dressing gown in front of a cable television series based in an American high school.

Sanvi is representative of a new Bombay breed: a young NRI returnee. She's undertaken the journey her parents took in reverse: born in New York, but returned to a 'homeland' she's never known, betting it all on her relevance to rising India's economic dream and her career as a student-cum-model and socialite.

Sanvi has one key bugbear about her adopted home, however, and it's one of the features Dimple and I are here to explore: Bombay's India-wide reputation for the flesh trade.

'Why did he do it? They are like soooo gross,' Sanvi asks a few days later, between mouthfuls of pakora and Coca-Cola and over the cheery refrain of the kids from *Glee* on Star World.

I blink. I'm coming round from the shock of waking to the sight of a huge black raven flying off with a pair of hand-washed knickers I'd strung to dry on the balcony outside my room; I'd wondered where the other two pairs had disappeared to. As I listen to Sanvi, I picture my practical smalls cushioning a raven's Bombay high rise.

'With their cheap clothes and their cheap conversation and all that disgusting flubber hanging out,' Sanvi continues. 'They freak me out. But they don't freak the NRI guys out. You know what? The guys get titillated. They deserve it when the bitches give them HIV; or they bleed them dry and don't even sleep with them.'

Today, it's this one particular manifestation of sleazy Bombay that's incensed Sanvi. Her most recent ex, a hi-fi media mogul based between Bombay and London, has just been, as she sees it, 'hoodwinked' by an aspirant Bollywood actress he met at a pool party in Juhu. Sanvi has decided that this contender for her ex's affections is like many of the ambitious girls from India and now, increasingly, the West who spill into Bombay's western suburbs: a 'shady person' willing to sleep her way up the ladder via the casting couch, or, in that Indian term that implies dancing-girl-cum-prostitute, a 'bar girl'.

Many of the thousands of new arrivals to Bombay feed the city's vicious appetite for flesh: for flesh to clean apartments three times a day against the thick film of dust that settles on everything, kicked up by the ever-gridlocked streets; and for flesh to feed New India's sexual appetite. The city is home to Asia's most famous red light district, and is where the divide blurs between young boys and girls hoping to make it in Bollywood and those willing to turn tricks for a quick rupee.

An illustration of the blurred line between Bombay's bright lights and its insalubrious back alleys came in early 2013, in the case of a female sex racketeer named Tina Umesh Deshpande. The 44-year-old was charged with summoning a string of aspirant models to her Bombay bungalow on the pretext of a modelling shoot. Once there, Kalyani allegedly coerced the girls into having sex with male 'customers' whom she had charged 80,000 rupees a head. The game was up for Deshpande when a 23-year-old model reported her for locking her up in a room inside the same bungalow for 48 hours after refusing to have sex with two men.

In Bombay's press of human flesh – from prostitutes and pimps to racketeers and gym-addicted muscle boys – the bar girls are one group who are as visible as they are vilified. From the early 2000s, these erotic dancers-lite became synonymous with the sleazier appetites of the city, loudly denounced by a conservative Maharastran state leadership and its police force. Yet compared to the strip clubs in the West, their offering was rather tame.

Drawing on Middle Eastern belly dance but also on the ancient Indian dance traditions of the tawaifs and mujra dancers, the bar girls titillated by suggestion. They danced with veils and scarves and remained largely clothed throughout the performance, excepting flashes of exposed flesh on their midriff, back and arms. Sometimes there would be a hijra dance for variety. Men would sit at tables drinking whisky, eating and ogling. Intermittently they'd throw rupee notes onto the stage towards girls they fancied; this lucre was collected in boxes by attendants and distributed between the girls and the management at the end of the night.

But Bombay's bar girls became the focus of the reactionary politicking of conservative Hindu nationalists. The tipping point came in 2005, when Maharastra brought in a Police Amendment Bill banning 'dance bars', the adult entertainment and strip-dance venues out of which most of the bar girls operated. At the point of the ban, over 700 dance bars were in operation in Bombay (305 of them officially registered). These establishments employed 75,000 girls as strip-dancers, with some unlicensed operations also acting as fronts for prostitution, sex trafficking and the drug trade.

After the ban, a number of Bombay's bar girls were trafficked to Dubai. Others continued to operate out of clandestine dance bars that sprang up in the outer and northern suburbs, such as the underground club in Juhu that supplied the girls for the pool party recently attended by Sanvi's ex.

Today, the Maharastran police crackdowns, which echo those of the Victorian Raj in their moralising vehemence, have a new front of attack: Bombay's club- and bar-going youth. In 2012, police commissioner Vasant Dhoble ordered a series of raids on the city's bars and nightclubs, shutting down hundreds of popular establishments for infringements ranging from overcrowding to failing to comply with the many licences needed to run a venue. Dhoble also set about enforcing the archaic Bombay Prohibition Act of 1952, which requires people to be issued with, and display, paper permits should they wish to consume alcohol at home or in a bar.

To many young Bombayites, Dhoble's campaign is seen not as a moral crusade, but as an opening salvo in a war between modern attitudes and those of the increasingly ardent Hindu traditionalists. In June 2012, during a break from the monsoon rains, hundreds of young Bombayites took to Juhu beach to protest against Dhoble's raids. Many wore black, that taboo Hindu colour, to mourn what they claimed to be the death of nightlife in the city. Others held hockey sticks on which were written 'Dhoble go back', a reference to the police commissioner's habit of carrying hockey sticks on his raids. They chanted: 'We want to be free! We want to be free!'

Away from likely encounters with former in-laws, Dimple had been looking forward to letting her hair down in India's buzziest metro. But we were also aware of Bombay's 'party pooper' and had discussed him while sitting on the tarmac of his city's airport. Dimple had bemoaned the new anti-youth mood that Dhoble's raids represent.

'The Hindu right and their myth of a gilded Hindu past, it drives me crazy!' she said. 'They lay into kids and they lay into women. They peddle all that propaganda about the "traditional woman" as a mother, as a keeper of traditions and the person without whom the family would fall apart.

'My ex father-in-law was full of it. The stereotype is as restrictive as a cheap saree blouse. It's almost like, if you're a woman, either you're that ideal, and you're approved of, or you do something you like with your life, and you're responsible for ruining India.'

'The dance bars served an important function in Bombay,' says Rajendar Menen, a Chennai-born journalist who refers to himself as a 'professional Bombay street bum'.

'Bombay is a city that's about business,' he continues. 'Most business transactions in India involve payments under the table, and ladies bars are a good way to get rid of the money that can't be stored in banks: the black money. The money found its way into the pockets of women with no education, and no other way of earning money to live. So, when the bars closed, thousands of women lost their livelihood and slipped into the flesh industry in the furthest corners of the city. Their only currency now is sex...

'And sex workers have a short shelf-life. They have to mint the moment.'

The son of well-to-do Tamils, but keen to make his own way in life, Menen arrived in Bombay in the late 1980s with a few rupees to his name, slept rough and caught, among other things, a bug for pacing its streets. From the early 1990s, he worked as a reporter for a national newspaper based out of Bombay, with prostitution and the criminal underworld as his beat. Later he worked as a fixer for the international NGOs battling the HIV epidemic that was laying siege to India's oldest (and Asia's second largest) red-light district: Kamathipura, in central Bombay.

Unsurprisingly Menen, now 50, is a hard-bitten, seen-it-all kind of guy. We meet him at nightfall at one of his favourite stamping grounds: Juhu Beach.

This forms the outer fringe of the fashionable northern suburbs: a crinoline of white-beige sands combed by the turbulence of the commercial airliners taking off from nearby Sahar International airport.

By night, Juhu is enlivened by chai stalls; hawkers selling giant balloons and candyfloss; and soliciting prostitutes catering to every sexual tastebud: children (sometimes orphans, sometimes youngsters pushed into the trade by their parents), small Bihari women, camp boys and hijras. For decades, Juhu Beach, along with Girgaum chowpatty beach further south, has been a key Bombay tourist destination, a rare chance to take a breather away from the uncompromising inland crush of bodies, buildings and nose-to-tail autos.

It all changed for Juhu Beach in November 2008, when 50 Pakistani terrorists gained land at Bombay in inflatable speedboats, having sailed from Karachi and hijacked an Indian trawler en route. Cocaine and steroid drugged and armed with incendiary bombs and AK-47 rifles, they went on a three-day killing spree that resulted in 166 fatalities. Indian authorities now attribute the attack to Pakistani terrorist organisation Lashkar-e-Taiba.

In the aftermath of the Bombay bombings, the Indian government promised a wholesale overhaul of the city's military and police protection mechanisms. However, few Bombayites trust that efficiency will win out over the city's dyed-in-the-wool corruption. Most fear that terrorists will come again and, when they do, will land via Bombay's beaches and ports – and the result is that tourists and fun-seeking Bombayites don't come to Juhu Beach in the numbers they once did.

'Strugglers still come here, though,' says Menen.

We've taken a seat on the sands in front of a rustic chai stall run by one of Menen's friends, a wiry man from Uttar Pradesh who wears a stained white muscle T-shirt and checked dhoti.

It's now dark, the sky lit by a waning crescent moon; before us, the Arabian Sea is a fathomless navy blue. The chai is cloyingly sweet.

'Who are the strugglers?' I ask Menen.

'The strugglers are the boys or girls who come from the small towns in India where Hindi cinema is the only thing that gives people reason to live. You've got 260 million illiterates in India, remember? Half of Indians shit outside, but

47 per cent have a TV at home. So they congregate around their shared TV and you give them what they want.

'What they want is Bollywood and rippling torsos and jiggling bosoms. You give them Katerina Kaif with her toushie out and 300 million boys masturbate.

'And what happens then?' he continues. 'Naturally you give them dreams of becoming their screen heroes. They're mesmerised. So they come to Bombay with no connections. Bombay is cruel to them; so they end up as prostitutes and gigolos, their looks fading along with their dreams. They come to the beach to recharge those failing dreams, to rehearse their Oscar acceptance speeches; sometimes just to find a bed for the night on the sand.'

Beside us on the beach, two wild dogs begin an energetic, and impeccably timed, bout of coitus. Dimple flinches. Rajendar observes them intently.

'Dogs, hookers, strugglers: they all have their territory around here,' he says. 'There are dogs like these and dogs they've castrated for population control. They get plump when they're castrated, like the hijra do.'

After a moment's silence, Menen continues. 'For sex workers, moonless nights like these are the busiest nights. Sexual excursions take place openly in the brush at the back of the beach. There's a big space crunch, so everyone understands.'

A small man passes by, a couple of greying towels slung over his left shoulder. Menen points at him. 'See this man? He's a masseur. Maailishwalas walk around with their bottles of oil and soiled bed sheets. They lay them out on the sand and perform foot massages or oil or dry body massages. Of course, there's more on offer if you want it. Homosexual sex, usually... It's all for sale at Juhu.'

Menen spits between his teeth towards the sea like a mafioso's gesture of disrespect, and then throws his spent plastic water bottle in the direction of the spit trail. He catches my flicker of disapproval.

'Remember, Sally, that Indians are the world's first and finest recyclers. I know a man will earn his dal and rice by walking up the beach later, collecting these bottles, selling them by the kay gee.

'It's time. Let's go,' he says.

It's 11 p.m. when Menen, Dimple and I reach the underbelly of modern Bombay. It takes us 20 minutes to find a cab driver willing to drive us there; most look us up and down, with narrowed eyes, then quickly drive away.

'They think you're prize prostitutes and I'm your pimp,' says Menen, his smile showing how much he enjoys this idea.

Kamathipura was the underbelly of old Bombay, too. One of the low-lying marshes created by the land-reclamation projects of the late eighteenth century, the quarter was first home to migrant workers from Andra Pradesh. By the 1880s, Kamathipura had developed the personality it has today, having become an official 'comfort zone' for British troops in the Raj army. Other areas of Bombay housed more prostitutes by number, but it was at Kamathipura that the consorts were understood to be at their most exotic.

As we saw at Shimla, marriage was frowned on for lower-ranking soldiers in Raj-era India. So the choice, as the British authorities saw it, was between two evils: the increasing of marriage quotas, leading to the expense of marriage allowances and family quarters; or condoning the 'deplorable evils' of inter-barrack sodomy and prostitution, the latter coming with the concomitant risk of a venereal disease epidemic caused by the 'sand rag' brothels of the Indian bazaars.

The only solution, in the mind of Viceroy Elgin, was to establish 'regimental brothels'. Through the late 1890s, Elgin regulated prostitution in 75 cantonments and set up 2000 lock hospitals to treat prostitutes with venereal disease, as well as a servicing army of travelling Indian prostitutes in regimental brothels, or chaklas, who were reserved, supposedly, for white male use. By the early 1900s it was impossible, said Frank Richards, a soldier stationed at Agra in the early 1900s, to leave barracks without being offered a 'jiggy-jig'. For many men, sexual sport with Indian prostitutes was an antidote to the loneliness of the soldier's life; indeed, for some it was an antidote to the type of women they might have met back home.

There was a marked taste, too, among these men for these 'succulent houris of the East'. Captain Edward Sellon, a writer and translator of erotica, describes the kid-in-a-sweetshop gusto with which he threw himself into liaisons with Indian women during the ten years (from 16 to 26 years old) in which he served in the Indian Army. In his diaries and correspondence he praises the 'cleanliness, dress, temperance and feminine accomplishments' of high-class Indian courtesans.

Indeed, prostitution was a much more honourable occupation in India than it was in the capital city of the British Empire back in London. Asian prostitutes, including the pliant Hindus and the crème de la crème, the Japanese prostitute, were erudite and playful hostesses, trained for their art. In the 1900s, an Anglo-Indian prostitute, her name unrecorded, announced her retirement at 50, after 36 years' service. She kept an open house for four hours where 'enormous numbers' turned out to pay her their respects.

Meanwhile, British prostitutes of the time were considered unexportable on the sex-trafficking routes (which spiderwebbed across the globe and were expanded after the opening of the Suez Canal) due to a 'degraded character' and ignorance of the finer skills (that is, oral and anal) of their trade. In the diaries of another Indian Raj soldier, G.R., we learn that after mastering the 'Indian method' he found himself able to 'open the eyes' of white European lovers as to the pleasures and possibilities of sex. It didn't work both ways with regard to the enjoyment of sex between white men and Indian women, though. Indian women seldom thought much of British men as lovers, considering them nonchalant and insensitive to female sexual needs.

Burton makes a similar distinction between Eastern and Western sex workers in his introduction to the Kama Sutra's Book Six, On Courtesans (which, as we've seen, is tellingly respectful to the Gupta Empire's courtesan class):

> *The Hindus have ever had the good sense to recognize courtesans as a part and portion of human society and, so long as they behaved themselves with decency and propriety, they were regarded with certain respect. They have never been treated with that brutality and contempt so common in the West, while their education has always been of a superior kind to that bestowed upon the rest of womankind in Oriental countries.*

It's a different story for the sex workers of modern India.

⁂

The streets of Kamithpura seem freighted with this colourful history. In the pale light bleeding from the open doorways of its shabby low rises, I can make out the silhouettes of small women in sarees, a few in Western clothes, alongside taller forms in exaggerated female poses: the telltale lineaments of the hijra. Knots of men stand around at the streetside, in darkness, while a few desultory women, more scantily dressed, sit on the loose and jutting stones of the kerb.

Our taxi had left us near to central Bombay station, at the edge of the district, so we're on foot. There's a definite air of menace in the air and – unusually for me – I'm feeling nervous.

'You two, stay close to me,' says Menen. 'They don't see white people down here that much, apart from white tourists ogling from taxis. But those never get out, unless they're buying.'

'How do they get cabs to drive around here?' I ask, remembering our struggle.

'They pay four times the going rate. Or they transfer at Bombay Central into the Kamathpura fleet. They're the cabs that work this district, turning a blind eye to sex acts in the back seat. I don't much like to sit on those seats, as you can imagine.'

'How much do these girls charge?' asks Dimple in low tones.

'These days,' continues Menen, 'the girls cost 100 rupees. It's gone down since the AIDS epidemic. You have to think, that's less than a coffee at one of the uptown coffee shops. The charge is more at Congress House across town. There the girls come from the old tawaif families, or they have very white skin; they can usually speak English. A businessman can pick up a Congress girl and take her to a party as his girlfriend. She'll charge up to 10,000 rupees for the privilege. But it's very different here at Kamithpura.'

'Is the AIDS epidemic under control?' I ask.

'Yes, the HIV message has got through,' Menen rejoins. 'The girls call it "AIDSee". I ask them, "Do you have sex without a condom, if it's a clean-looking man?" They say "no", firmly; they know you can't see AIDSee.

'I used to stay overnight in one of the brothels on this street in my old reporting days,' he continues, pointing to a narrow thoroughfare to our immediate right. Close up, at the head of the road, a small spry man stands, smoking a strong-smelling clove cigarette that's clamped between his two remaining front teeth.

'The thing about prostitutes – about any Indians who are on their knees – is that they'll give you their last chapatti. There was one girl working this street, Sumitra I'll call her. She'd had razorblades put to her throat on too many occasions to mention; she'd had one of her nipples sliced off by a client... But still she would cook a homely meal for me, in a small kitchen behind the bed where she serviced her clients. She'd lend me her last 50 rupees if I needed it. She made me cry with gratitude.'

'How had she come to be in Kamithpura?' I say, as we follow our guide onto a better-lit main street that's filled with parked cab drivers shooting the breeze.

'You know what, Sally,' says Menen, 'the story is the same for most of the Kamithpura girls. She's a girl who comes from nothing. She'll get raped at 12 unless she's married, probably by a family member. So she's married off young; at least if she's married her baby is legitimised.

'When she's 15 her 20-year-old husband leaves her. He goes to another city to look for work, or to live out his youth. He leaves her with no money and a kid to support. So what does she do? She goes into prostitution, probably in a big city where no one knows her. She leaves the kid with her mother, sends all of her earnings back. She tells herself she'll do it for a few years, earn enough to set up a business back home, or find a husband. But she doesn't. She gets stuck here in Kamithpura. Her kid doesn't know her. And she earns less and less, of course, working against the tick-tick-ticking clock of her fading looks.'

Another blight on these girls' desperate lives, and it's one shared by India's rape victims, is the struggle to achieve justice against civil service corruption. Take this, the anonymous complaint of an Indian sex worker to the *Hindustan Times* in the wake of the 2013 rape uprisings:

> *My most cruel assaulters are often the men in uniform. Yes, the cops who blackmail us to pay bribes so that we can carry on with our jobs as sex workers. Refusal to please them means lathis [beatings with Indian truncheons], kicks in the mouth, abuses and, finally, rape... I have often been raped by cops in parks, and even inside lock-ups. Some often stop me on the road and ask for a quick oral sex. Even when I step out from home for personal work, they insist on sex. Any resistance is met with abuses and torture. At times, I try and run away from the cops. I once bit their hand in a bid to escape.*

Menen leads us into an ancient-looking chai house that's filled with autorickshaw drivers. They're all in their uniforms of beige polyester shirts and trousers, some in mismatched shades of cream-beige. Forty pairs of eyes bore into us.

Seeing us, the owner, a middle-aged Muslim with a vibrant, henna-dyed beard, leaps up and wipes a table down for us, with a dingy rag.

'What happens next?' I ask Menen. 'When her looks fade, I mean?'

'If she's shrewd she becomes a madam,' he explains. 'Some girls become cleaners in brothels. Many die of disease. Not just venereal: there's a big problem with tuberculosis in Kamithpura. The lucky, and rare, ones will marry a customer. When I worked with NGOs here a few of the white guys from the US and Europe married prostitutes. I keep in touch with two of the couples. They're happy, you know, all things considered.'

He lifts an index finger, signalling the owner to bring us three cups of chai. 'Nine rupees it costs for chai now,' he says, 'used to be five. Gone up four rupees in five years... Incredible India, eh?'

All eyes continue to burrow into us, apart from those belonging to a man at an adjacent table. He has a shrunken right arm. With four webbed fingers he's scooping dal into his mouth, using half a chapatti as a shovel.

The tea arrives, served by the red-bearded man, slopped onto the table unceremoniously. I notice a couple of young men with shaved heads in the far corner of the room and ask Menen about them.

'They're marines,' he says, as he noisily slurps his chai. 'They will get into a lot of trouble with their superiors if they're known to be here at Kamithpura.

'Look at them. They're staring at you. Shall I tell you what they're thinking? All they're thinking about is how they'd like to fuck you. That's what women don't understand. Young men have this snake in their pants; it's all they can think about. It's all I ever thought about until I got to my 40s. It makes us imbeciles. We can't function; so why do Indian families treat young men like gods? They're imbeciles!'

We're distracted now by a hijra sashaying past the café window, all long limbs and self-assuredness. Her face is scarred and coated in yellow-looking make-up.

'I saw a hijra castration once, you know,' confides Menen, 'in one of the brothels around here. The Dai Mas, or senior eunuchs, perform it.'

'I've always wanted to know what happens,' says Dimple.

I'd always wanted to know, too. Now, as Menen starts to answer, I'm not so sure I do.

'The patient will fast and pray for ten days to the Goddess Amba and castration is performed on the eleventh day with those attending the ceremony standing naked,' he tells us.

'The operation is primitive: a little alcohol, but no anaesthesia to numb the pain. The penis and testicles are sliced off the body with a knife, or a black silk thread; then hot oil is poured on the wound to stop the bleeding. Next they insert a neem stick into the opening to the urethra to prevent it closing, and hot oil is poured down this opening.

'It sounds gory, but there's a beautiful spiritual beauty to the ritual. It's like delivering a new child. On the sixth day, the eunuch will be given her new name.'

We sit silently for a minute or so, contemplating this.

'You girls, you look depressed. But I no longer get depressed about these facts of life,' said Menen.

'I read an interview with Madonna a couple of years ago. As a teenager she fucked for profit, for her career, to hang out with rich guys; she had no shame in admitting it. And what are most Indian marriages but legalised prostitution? It's only the lucky girls in India who get to afford the luxury of shame. It's the same story everywhere.

'Eight million people a day use Bombay trains, and one million people fuck for a living. That's just the way it is...'

15 | LOVE BYTES, Bombay

The world's busiest matchmakers – and the online love sleuth

One who relates to both partners, and is open-minded towards both, specially the woman; such a person can be used with confidence as the messenger. The qualities desirable in such a person are eloquence, pertness, an understanding of the signals of emotion, a knowledge of the right time for deception, a feel for what is possible, quick grasp and resourcefulness.

—Kama Sutra, Book One, General,
A.N.D. Haksar translation, 2011

Oh pearl of the nose-ring, thrice blessed are you; there is no limit to your good fortune!
No enquiries have been made into your lineage, your rank, and yet day or night you taste the nectar of her lips.

—Bihari Lal (1595–1663), Mughal poet

A week later and we have an appointment with a Bombayite who trades in those ancient commodities of love and lust on a global scale. Dimple's excited by the prospect of meeting the man behind the marital matchmaking site Shaadi.com (shaadi being Hindi for wedding).

'I see it among my younger cousins,' she tells me excitedly, as we sit in a taxi in rush-hour traffic, battling the long slog south along the Bombay peninsula in the daily bumper-to-bumper grind.

A young, barefoot hawker boy presses himself against the window; the lowest rung of entrepreneurship in this nation of tooth-and-claw entrepreneurs. I notice, with a smile, that he's selling pirate editions of *Steve Jobs: An Autobiography*.

'I had little choice, and no power, when it came to choosing my match,' continues Dimple. 'But my cousins, they're 10, 15 years younger, and it's all in their hands. They say: 'Ammi, we will find a good homely boy, an engineer, Ammi; we will do it on Shaadi,' and Ammi agrees, as she cannot use the internet, and the village matchmakers are going down, so her daughter has the power, for the first time in, aaah, a thousand years.'

Anupam Mittal, the man behind Shaadi.com, tells us, 'We overtook the newspaper classifieds, and the village matchmakers and pandits [religious teachers], oh, a decade ago.'

We meet this urbane, dedicated bachelor in the rookery-like central Bombay offices of People Interactive, also home to relationship advice portal ShaadiTimes; social networking site Fropper.com; and Astrolife.com, an online astrology service provider.

But it's Shaadi.com that heads up this successful portfolio of online networking businesses. Mittal launched the site from his student bedroom in the US in the mid-1990s. Today, he controls 40 per cent of India's US$1 billion per annum online matchmaking industry and has, at current count, arranged the marriage matches of two million couples of South Asian descent.

'In some ways young Indians want the same things they always did,' Mittal says. 'They want companionship. They want a marriage that's the union of two families...

'But in other ways we, as Indians, have changed beyond recognition. Love-cum-arranged-marriages are more the norm. And Indian women are becoming more confident. They might not go to bars to pick men up; but they do want a say in finding their mate. Online matchmaking facilitates this. Whereas before, a local matchmaker would find them a husband from a handful of local candidates, now they have a vast canvas of potential mates across India... across the world.'

In the last available figures, from 2011, 42 per cent of India's 45 million internet users were signed up to a matrimonial matching site, from market leaders Shaadi.com and BharatMatrimony.com to more esoteric propositions, including a site dedicated to lovelorn eunuchs and one to Bramacharya celibates. This echoes the online matchmaking revolution in the West, where in 2011 statistics for the UK, one in five couples that marry will have met online. For many users in India, online matrimony will be their first experience of using the web; for other, sophisticated second-generation NRI users in the UK and US, the site represents an efficient way to seek out a pavaan, or homely, traditional bride.

Mittal arcs his computer screen round on its tripod and scrolls through the latest additions to his site: a batch of disembodied male heads, with bright eyes and uncertain smiles.

'What's fascinating,' he says, 'is how much you can read by communities' preferences. The Brahmins in rural Tamil Nadu, for example, only want a match from among the Tamil Brahmin caste, whereas Indians in the big metros are broadening their tastes. Here we can see the old, rigid caste preferences of thousands of years beginning to shift.'

But the real sign of the times, he explains, is seen in the waning preference for non-resident Indians. 'In the early days of Shaadi.com, grooms in the UK and US were still a hot commodity. All the girls wanted to marry a doctor in the UK, a tech guy in California. Today, all of that's changed. If the future is in India, why does a young girl want to leave her family and go overseas? If you'll excuse the acronyms, the NRI men have lost their USP.'

To negotiate this imbroglio of market forces and cultural preferences, Mittal has trained a team of crack matchmakers, who are expected to speak a minimum of three Indian languages and to be up to date in the mercurial tastes of Shaadi.com's clientele. Mittal walks me through the warrens of cubbyhole offices to meet 40-something Gayartri Kapoor, one of the most experienced of these new-fashioned cupids, a friendly, mumsy sort who's wearing thick-framed spectacles.

'This job gives me the goosebumps,' she tells me, when I ask how she ended up in this singular twenty-first-century vocation. 'For many of my clients I become part of the family; and I've been invited to so many weddings I've lost count. But actually, it's tough. I need to be a therapist and an anthropologist rolled into one. Only this morning I had to spend an hour reading up on the beliefs of a specific sub-branch of unshaved Sikhs in the Punjab. Sometimes the client's parents have put them on the site, so I have to gently explain what the internet means to nervous parents.'

Indian parents do have cause to worry about the implications of this brave new matrimonial medium. In 2012, a US report found that one in three profiles on free dating websites are fake, with a further third being inaccurate to a greater or lesser degree. Much of Shaadi.com's product development, Mittal tells me now, is geared towards rooting out fake or inaccurate profiles.

Despite this fact, we apparently instinctively trust online matches. Research conducted in the US finds that Western couples who meet online typically move in with each other earlier: at seven months into the relationship, compared to 18 months for couples who meet by other means. Perhaps for the same reason, their relationships often dissolve more quickly than unions forged by more traditional means: a poor average of eight months.

So what, I ask Mittal, are the preoccupations of Shaadi.com's users?

'The girls will say they're modern but homely, with white or wheatish skin,' he says. 'And of course the men are always several inches taller on the internet than in real life; many more of them have PhDs than we know graduate from Indian colleges with the same. But what they don't know is that we use complex probability algorithms. So if we have a spike of 6 ft tall Indians, we know that something is amiss.'

As well as tackling the mendacity that appears to be endemic among matchmaking website users in East and West alike, Mittal sees it as his business to update outmoded marital practices.

'Dowries are still a big problem for India,' he continues. 'Officially the practice of exacting a large dowry is illegal in most states. A few years ago there was a spate of high-profile dowry murders, where men had killed their brides within months of marriage, when they had the dowry in their hands. So many states brought in statutes to ban large dowries, or to ban dowries completely. Of course, the reality is that the dowry tradition continues, and its consequences can be extreme: female infanticide by parents who can't afford the dowry for a daughter; families going bankrupt because the price of trousseau gold has quadrupled.'

Despite the dowry practice being outlawed, related crimes are routine in India, with researchers estimating that between 25,000 and 100,000 women a year are killed over dowry disputes. Many are burned alive in a grisly form of retribution that intentionally echoes the practice of sati, the ritual self-immolation of a widow on her husband's funeral pyre.

In early 2012, Shaadi.com decided to tackle the issue in a novel way. It created an internet meme called 'Angry Brides', inspired by the fad Facebook game 'Angry Birds'.

'It's a game accessed, in the same way, through Facebook,' Mittal says. 'Players control a many-armed bride who can hurl shoes, veggies, even knives, at dowry-seeking targets. It's great fun!'

Before Dimple and I leave Mittal and Kapoor to tend to their 40 million-plus lonely hearts, I ask them where I'd rank, in India's largest love shop, as a 5 ft 9 in, 30-something single white woman.

Kapoor's lip curves into a lopsided smile. 'For a first marriage you'd have a problem with age, of course; and your height, too. Perhaps a divorced man in one of the big cities?'

'It all depends,' laughs Dimple. 'What are your chapattis like?'

We head on to meet another character who could only have emerged from the preoccupations, in love and lust, of modern India.

Vikas Sharma, a long-time private investigator for Bombay-based security provider Topsgrup, works a beat that Anupam Mittal's algorithms cannot reach. Sharma is India's premier and self-styled 'love sleuth', making a good living researching the veracity of the advertisements of India's homely girls and their 6 ft suitors.

'For a couple of decades, I'd been doing the usual PI work,' Sharma explains, over coffee at a business hotel in Sahar, near to Bombay's international airport. 'Corporate stuff mainly, researching corrupt employees for their bosses, that kind of thing. It was in the mid-2000s that I began to get commissions for matrimonial work, usually parents looking into potential sons-in-law, sometimes the bride or the groom themselves.'

Sharma falls silent while the waiter pours three coffees from a steaming cafetière, then he continues. 'Early on I had this guy in Pune who was engaged to a girl in Bombay. They'd been matched online. He said he was this hotshot businessman and he'd met his bride-to-be a few times in Bombay, with her parents. He'd taken the whole family to a car showroom, put a deposit cheque down on a Mercedes. Next time he did the same with a flash apartment – took his new bride to see it, put down a deposit cheque of several lakhs.

'Thing was,' he continues, 'it was just for show... all the cheques were bouncing. I found this out from following his trail around the property agents and showrooms, and through two weeks of surveillance in Pune. He was playing all of these girls from rich families off against each other, looking for a bride with a dowry big enough to pay off his gambling debt.'

'He had his eyes on the prize,' Dimple laughs. 'That's a very old idea in Indian matchmaking, as my mother would tell you.'

'Yes,' says Sharma. 'But what I didn't expect was the extent of these cases. Now since 2010 I mainly undertake matrimonial work. And in 80 per cent of cases the party who employs me has very good reasons for their suspicion. Usually the groom has lied about his job or educational achievements. Sometimes the bride is divorced and has kept this fact from the groom.'

For a fee of US$100, Sharma offers his clients an investigation package that includes internet research, as well as old fashioned on-the-ground surveillance and photography. He promises to illuminate, as his company advertisements put it, 'social reputation, family background, business status, vices, medical and education history and past broken/ unbroken marriages'.

Our coffee cups drained, Dimple looks thoughtful. 'Let me tell you,' she says, 'in my mother's day there was a local matchmaker, a very good one. She matched my parents, and my grandparents before them, and she made it her business to know all of the dirty laundry. There was this rumour that she used to go through the rubbish of the families she was matching.'

'Of course, you can see my work in the same way as the old village matchmakers,' Sharma responds, smiling. 'It's the same thing, on a bigger scale. I'm that man in the shadows, searching the garbage for India's dirty secrets.'

As we leave him and begin one of the daily rate negotiations of a taxi fare with another of this breathless twenty-first-century city's entrepreneurs, I consider this portrait of the new internet union. Clearly, the new world order is offering never-before-seen freedoms to young Indians empowered, for the first time, to seek their own marital match. But it's also created a world in which our online identities are flexible, and often outright fallacious, and enabled a boon for fraudsters pushing scams to lonely, sometimes desperate people looking for love online.

The full implications of the crashing together of the world's online and offline love lives has yet to play out, in either the East or the West. It will take a generation before the ramifications of this paradigm shift in the way we meet and marry are understood – what this networked world might mean for our pursuit and expressions of love and lust.

However, perhaps there are reasons to be cheerful about this parallel universe peopled by chameleon personalities and love-lorn souls. According to a 2005 study, 'Identity Recreation via Internet Dating' by Jennifer Yurchisin of Iowa State University, there are advantages in this tendency of internet dating sites to turn us into character chameleons.

'We know that, compared to conventional methods, internet-dating services perform poorly in terms of matchmaking and long-term relationship formation,' says Yurchisin. 'What we find is that much of the popularity of internet matchmaking is in the process. Posting profiles and responding to feedback to emphasise certain aspects of our personality is a powerful tool in learning who we are now – and who we have the potential to become.'

16 | TEN THOUSAND BIG, FAT INDIAN WEDDINGS

Bombay and beyond...

The notion of romantic love has erected impassable barriers between us and the classical past, or Oriental present.

—CS Lewis, The Allegory of Love

What are the sins of my race, Beloved,
What are my people to thee?
And what are thy shrines, and kine and kindred
What are they gods to me?
Love recks not of feuds or bitter follies,
Of stranger, comrade, or kin,
Alike in his ear sound the temple bells
And the cry of the muezzin.
For love shall cancel the ancient wrong
And conquer the ancient rage,
Redeem with his tears the memoried sorrow
That sullied a bygone age.

—An Indian Love Song, Sarojini Naidu, 1917

There's a commotion of banging, crashing and yelping going on outside the brass-studded teak of the Bombay villa door. Inside that same door, Dimple and I are arrayed in our finery. Dimple is in a rainbow of gem-studded pink and teal; I wear the vibrant red dress and pink-red dupatta she's coaxed me into, inducing me to cast aside the shalwar kameez that serves as my first line of defence against wandering Indian hands.

The lavish racket, just reaching its crescendo of arhythmic drumming after 45 minutes, is our host's bharat: the kick-off of a Hindu wedding ceremony, derived from a Sikh tradition, where the groom's wedding party, headed by his young male companions, ceremonially march to the bride's door in an inversion of that Western tradition of the bride walking down the aisle.

As India's wealth and confidence have burgeoned, so too have the pomp and vociferousness of the bharat. Today it can last up to three hours, with grooms arriving amid the bedlam on horseback; or, in a faddish new take on the tradition seen in the north of India, with the groom's party arriving atop quad roller skates. The competitive exhibitionism of the twenty-first-century bharat has led to the attendant phenomena, much bewailed by the Indian press, of bharat pickpockets and wedding crashers, the latter slipping into high-society wedding parties unseen in the brouhaha of the whole event.

Inside the villa door, Dimple and I stand on a tomato-red velvet carpet, dappled by the light of decorative lanterns, strung above and ordered at great expense from an avant-garde Bombay designer. We are serving chiefly decorative purposes, standing as we are in an area reserved for the out-of-town guests invited to exhibit the bride's cosmopolitanism and wealth, at the tail end of a patient guard of honour of family and friends.

As we stand here, tens of thousands across India are doing the same thing: glossily dressed wedding guests, neurotic parents and nervous newlyweds. Today is one of the season's most auspicious days for marriage, just one of a handful of dates against which Indian families clamour to book caterers and pandits, hoping to give their sons and daughters the best chance, astrologically speaking, of marital bliss.

Some of these thousands of couples will be like the young pair soon to be united by this opened door: a love-cum-arranged-marriage of a Western-educated couple, keen for a starring role in India's twenty-first-century success story. Others will never have met each other before their wedding day, the bride's head humbly bowed in silence and subordination beneath a heavy red ghoonghat. Still others will have chosen their own spouse online, an idea that would have been unconscionable for most Indian families even just a decade ago. Hundreds of these couples, perhaps thousands, might divorce in the years ahead, as the modern Western focus on individualism and self-fulfilment takes deeper root in India's ancient soil.

The heavy doors are thrown open to a flourish of drum roll, and the wedding party, in its peacock plumage of bright silks, trails into an extravagantly fitted-out wedding hall. I gaze at the young couple now established on the stage for the first of the interminable ceremonies and blessings that characterise the Hindu wedding. They sit there humbly: bride pretty and patient, dripping in gold ornamentation; groom in a finely wrought kurta. I wonder how their love life will be in the years to come: more satisfying than mine, to date, as a woman from the contracepted, post-revolution West? More satisfying than Dimple's gruesome experience of conjugal copulation?

In these months of my sexploration, I've come to understand that Indians and Britons both are sharing our marital beds with the spectres of a moralising past. Yes, the British Empire planted itself in India with 'theological force', but it spread its venereal diseases with as much brio as it did its sermonising, and it devoured India's ancient erotica with more success than it spread the biblical word as to sexual propriety.

So I've learned that, for all of our contraceptive pills and 24/7 porn, the Western sexual revolution isn't the epilogue we Westerners often, and arrogantly, think it is; certainly not the end game in the immemorial tussle of boy-meets-girl. Western girls look at breast augmentation as a means to an end for a career in glamour modelling and the final prize of a football-playing spouse. Many Western, net-porn-bombarded kids are growing up as ignorant of the interrelationship of sex and love.

We were told we could have it all; but somehow, somewhere, we were had.

So as India takes its first, awkward steps towards its societal and sexual revolution, I hope that something of the optimism Dimple and I have encountered during our subcontinental sexploration becomes real – that India's sexual revolution will be infused with its ancient myth and spirituality, and with the inheritance of the great Indian love stories.

In the complex and beautiful courtly love literature that bloomed in North India during the late Middle Ages, Krishna is not the priapic eve-teaser we met earlier, but a paradigm of elegance and etiquette, a refined courtier and a consummate lover. In epic poems such as those of Keshava Dasa of Orcha (1555–1617), poet at the court of Rajput chief Vir Singh Deo (in modern-day Madya Pradesh), Krishna and his lover Radha become models for human lovers in their quarrels, their separations and reconciliation, and their candidly described sexual ecstasy. In these old stories the pathos, fury and laughter retain their power to speak to us today, and, in many ways, put the sanitised love stories pedalled by both Bollywood and Hollywood in the shade.

Here, for example, in Keshava Dasa's Kaviprita, a poem inspired by the months of the year, we hear the voice of a woman in love viewing the changing seasons through the rose-tinted lens of her passions and pleading with her lover not to take his leave:

> *The streams filled by the monsoon rains look lovely while rushing along to unite with the sea. The creepers cling lovingly to the trees. The restless lightning flashes all around while flirting with the clouds. The peacocks, with their shrill cries, announce the union of earth and sky. All lovers meet in this month of Shravana. Why then, my love, even think of going out?*

I hope that the new sexual story the land of the Kama Sutra tells itself will feature some of the depths of romantic feeling of the old courtly poets – that it might rediscover the deep sentiments that gave the world its finest physical embodiment of romantic love: the Taj Mahal. This luminous marble mausoleum, built in the seventeenth century on the emerald grasslands of Uttar Pradesh by mourning Mughal widower Emperor Shah Jahan, offers a reminder to all of us – East and West – of something transcendent in the love unions of mortals, something bigger than all of the petty squabbles and painful repressions that characterise today's gender relations.

Will India find enlightenment, for its brave new age, in the pages of the Kama Sutra? Somehow, I doubt it. For all the candid eye the Kama Sutra casts on the pleasures of coition; for all its insistence, still controversial on the subcontinent, that women might enjoy sex; and for all its chaotic, enlivening and perverse portfolio of sexual moves, there's something very important that's absent in its pages. Its sex is one-faceted: it's about an act rather than an interaction. In writing for the omnipotent 'man about town', it doesn't occur to Vatsyayana that in sexual union there might be something more profound to be enjoyed than the expert performance of sexual positions – that there might be real contact.

In Delhi, there are signs that something of Shah Jahan's romantic tenderness lives on. In the past couple of years, lovers in the Indian capital have taken to flying kites to exchange love dispatches. As dusk falls on clear summer nights, the messages flutter into the air: messages to girlfriends kept in by their fathers; secret love codes only to be deciphered by the intended eyes. It's a nod to another ancient Indian love story, that of the nineteenth-century Urdu love poet Mirza Ghalib who, according to legend, wrote his fine romantic couplets on kites and flew them to his lover, the dancer Chunna Jan.

Two hours later, and our young newlyweds have seven times encircled the Vedic yajna, the ceremonial fire thought to invoke the Aryan deities and cement human alliances. They've chanted, in the south Indian tradition, the mantra:

> *Now let us make a vow together. We shall share love, share the same food, share our strengths, share the same tastes. We shall be of one mind.*

My mouth filled with pani-puri canapés and my heart, suddenly, expanding with hope, I glance over at Dimple. She's standing across the room, looking beautiful in her silks, chatting animatedly to a handsome young man from Rajastan.

I catch her eye. And we smile.

> *When the wheel of sexual ecstasy is in full motion, there is no textbook at all, and no order.*
>
> —*Kama Sutra*

Kamapedia

Amba one of the forms of the goddess Durga the invincible, the fiercest of the Hindu goddesses. Traditionally associated with the hijra (q.v.) community.

ammi mother, mum (Urdu).

apsara a heavenly nymph, or Hindu spirit of the clouds or waters, common to Hindu and Buddhist mythology.

artha pursuit of material and/or financial prosperity and one of the four aims in Hindu life, or purusarthas, with kama, dharma and moksha (q.v.).

Aryan derived from the Sanskrit for 'noble', a racial grouping commonly used in the nineteenth century to describe peoples of Indo-European Eurasian heritage. It derives from the idea that the original speakers of the Indo-European languages and their descendants up to the present day constitute a distinctive race or subrace of the larger Caucasian race. Aryanism developed as a racial ideology that claimed that the Aryans were a master race, as seen in 1930s and 1940s Nazi ideology. In the Indian take on this, the Aryan race was cited as superior to the darker 'Dravidian' race.

Ayurveda a system of traditional medicine native to the Indian subcontinent with roots dating back 2000 years. Today a broad-brush term for complementary or alternative medicine. Two-thirds of Indians use Ayurveda for their primary health-care needs, although safety concerns have been raised after studies in the US found toxic levels of heavy metals such as lead, mercury and arsenic in 20 per cent of Indian-manufactured patent Ayurvedic medicines.

bachao help, or save me.

badmash rogue or ruffian.

bharat Indian marriage procession, usually cacophonous.

bhartiya nari the concept of an 'ideal Indian woman' with attributes that often include homeliness and white or wheatish (q.v.) skin.

bhel puri a savoury Indian snack made of puffed rice, vegetables and a tangy tamarind sauce.

bibi an Indian mistress, common-law wife or long-term consort to an Englishman in India, a tradition popularised in late nineteenth-century Calcutta.

BIG acronym for Bad Indian Girl, antonymous to GIG (q.v.). One who doesn't adhere to the behaviours expected of demure, homely Indian womanhood.

BJP Bharatiya Janata Party, or Indian People's Party, one of two major parties in the Indian political system, operating on a right-wing socio-religious platform. Established in 1980, it is India's second largest political party in terms of representation in the parliament and in the various state assemblies.

brahmacharya a stage of Hindu life between the ages of 14 and 20 years, during which time the Vedic sciences are studied and strict celibacy is practised.

brahmin the priest and scholar caste in traditional Hindu societies of India and Nepal. Brahmins are the highest of the four varnas, or castes, which rank humanity by their innate spiritual purity.

chadoor an outer garment or cloak with roots in sixth-century Persia. Today wearing this garment is one of the ways in which a Muslim woman can follow the Islamic dress code, or hijab.

chai Hindi-Urdu, Arabic and Persian term for the beverage brewed from the cured leaves of the tea plant (*Camellia sinensis*) and derived from Mandarin 'chá'. In India commonly served as a blend of black tea and Indian herbs and spices: masala chai.

chandelas an Indian clan found in central India who ruled much of that area for long periods between the tenth and thirteenth centuries.

channa, **chana** chickpea, a legume high in protein and used in many south Asian cuisines. Chana or gram flour is used to make pappadoms, bhajis and as a constituent of homemade beauty products.

chillum a straight conical pipe, traditionally made of clay, associated with wandering Hindu monks, or sadhus (q.v.).

Crowley, Aleister a late nineteenth-century English occultist, mystic and ceremonial magician whose teachings were later rediscovered by the 1960s and 1970s avant-garde. Espousing a form of libertarianism based on his rule of 'Do What Thou Wilt',

Crowley (1875–1947) was a pansexual and recreational drug experimenter who in 1889 published the controversial *White Stains*, a series of poems on gay and straight sex and sado-masochism. Later, as a key member of Ordo Templi Orientis, a renegade order based on freemasonry, Crowley became an advocate for the practice of ritualistic homosexual 'sex magick'.

Delhi Sultanates five Indo-Islamic kingdoms that ruled from Delhi from 1206–1526 CE.

devadasi a girl 'married' to a Hindu deity and dedicated to worship and service of the deity or a temple for the rest of her life. Originally, in addition to taking care of the temple and performing rituals, these women learned and practised classical Indian artistic traditions, enjoyed a high social status and would marry rich temple patrons and bear their children. The pinnacle of the devadasi tradition, and its status, was the tenth to eleventh centuries CE. During the British Raj, reformists worked towards outlawing the devadasi tradition on grounds that it supported prostitution. If this charge was not true of all nineteenth-century devadasis, it is true today. Despite the fact that the tradition was outlawed in 1988, a 2004 report by the Human Rights Commission found the practice to be still prevalent in Karnataka and Andra Pradesh and that around 46 per cent of devadasis relied on prostitution as their chief source of income.

devi a mother goddess with various manifestations and roles, especially that of consort to Shiva.

dharma duty, moral righteousness or ethics, and one of the four aims in Hindu life, or purusarthas, along with kama, artha and moksha (q.v.).

dhoti a traditional man's garment worn in India, Bangladesh and Nepal, formed from a rectangular piece of unstitched cloth knotted at the waist and resembling a long skirt.

Diwali a five-day Hindu festival, popularly known as the 'festival of lights', which falls between mid-October and mid-November in the Gregorian calendar.

Dravidian a term used to refer to diverse groups of people who natively speak languages belonging to the Dravidian family, mostly found in south India. Although modern genetic studies have proved that the concept of a Dravidian 'race' is erroneous (see David Reich, *Reconstructing Indian Population History*), the idea retains cultural currency, and is often conflated with supposed physical characteristics of the 'Dravidian race', including darker skin and a shorter, stockier frame. *See also* Aryan.

East India Company an English and (from 1707) British joint-stock company formed in 1600 for pursuing trade with the East Indies, but which ended up trading mainly with the Indian subcontinent, North-west frontier province and Balochistan. By the 1870s its functions had been fully absorbed into the official government machinery of the British Raj and its private armies had been nationalised by the British Crown.

ESP extrasensory perception, or sixth sense, involves reception of information not gained through the recognised physical senses, but sensed with the mind. The term was adopted by American psychologist Joseph Banks Rhin (1895–1980) to denote psychic abilities such as telepathy and clairvoyance.

eve-teasing a euphemism used in India, Bangladesh and Nepal for the public sexual harassment of women by men, with 'eve' a biblical reference to Eve, the first woman.

firangi, farangi thought to be derived from Franks, the term for the Germanic tribes who once occupied land in the Lower and Middle Rhine, now a prevalent term in south and southeast Asia for a (usually Caucasian) foreigner.

Ganesh, Ganesha, Ganesa one of the best-known and most worshipped gods in the Hindu pantheon. Readily distinguished by his elephant head, Ganesh is revered as the remover of obstacles and lord of beginnings.

ghat a term used in the north of India to refer to a series of steps leading down to a body of water, chiefly a holy river.

ghoonghat a veil or headscarf used to cover the head. An ornate red ghoonghat is often central to an Indian bride's wedding attire.

GIG acronym for Good Indian Girl, popularly (and sometimes derisively) used to refer to a girl who exhibits features prized by Indian society, such as modesty and homeliness. *See also* BIG.

Gupta Empire an ancient Indian empire that existed from approximately 350 to 550 CE and covered much of the Indian subcontinent. Peaceful and prosperous, the Gupta Empire is often held up as the Golden Age of India, when science and art flourished.

gurana a historical community of hijras (q.v.), often but not necessarily contained in one extended property.

Gurkha an indigenous people mainly from mid-western and eastern Nepal. Gurkhas fought against the East India Company (q.v.) in the 1814–16 Gurkha War. While the British-run East India Company won the war (with Nepal ceding two-thirds of its land), the Gurkhas were praised for their martial qualities and tenacity. Later they were commissioned as troops under contract to the East India Company and became part of the British Indian Army on its formation in 1895. During the Second World War 10 Gurkha regiments fought for the Allies.

halal foods that Muslims are allowed to eat under Islamic Shari'ah law. The criteria specify both what foods are allowed and how the food must be prepared.

haram both the opposite of halal (q.v.) and a broader Arabic term meaning 'sinful', used to refer to any act that is forbidden by god.

hijra third sex or third gender, physiological males who have feminine gender identity, adopt feminine gender roles and wear women's clothing. They may or may not be castrated and may or may not take gender-altering female hormones. In ancient Indian society as represented in the Kama Sutra, fellatio is traditionally performed by people of the third sex. Today many hijras live in organised, all-hijra communities under a teacher or guru. The communities sustain themselves by adopting young boys who are rejected by their families. Many hijras are sex workers.

Holi the Hindu spring festival or 'festival of colours', with rituals including the drenching of celebrants in coloured water.

Indian National Congress one of two major political parties in India, operating on a modern liberal platform. It is the largest and one of the oldest democratically operating political parties in the world, having been established by Indian and British members of the Theosophical Society in Madras in 1884.

item number in Indian cinema, a performance that has little to do with the film in which it appears but is presented to showcase a beautiful dancing girl, and increase the marketability of the film.

Jainism an Indian religion that prescribes a path of non-violence towards all living beings.

jarikar a form of textile work that includes a silk overlaid, pleated hem.

jat a community of traditionally non-elite herders and tillers from northern India and Pakistan. Today many jats work as long-distance truck drivers. Popularly depicted as macho.

Kali the Hindu goddess of time or change, often associated with blackness, death and regeneration. Also associated with Shakti (q.v.). Consort of Shiva.

kama a Sanskrit term that is often translated as sexual or sensual desire or eros, but can broadly mean desire, wish, passion or aesthetic enjoyment of life. One of the four goals of a Hindu life. Not to be confused with karma, the ancient Indian concept of cause and effect.

Kama Sutra the most notable of a group of texts generically known as Kama Shastra, or 'discipline of Kama'. Believed to be written by an ascetic called Vatsyayana. Contrary to popular opinion in the West, not merely a sex manual, but a guide to virtuous and gracious living that discusses the nature of love, family life and other aspects pertaining to the pleasure-oriented faculties of human life. The intended audience of the text is the moneyed man about town of the Gupta Empire. Believed to be written at some point between 400 BCE and 200 CE.

khap panchayat a body of local governance, a council of five, which typically governs a village unit.

Kundalini the concept, in Tantra and yoga, of a dormant corporeal energy or 'coiled beast'. Described in some modern commentaries as an unconscious, instinctive or libidinal force. Certain hatha yoga practices aim to awaken the Kundalini force.

lakh unit in the south Asian numbering system equal to one hundred thousand.

Lakshmi the Hindu goddess of wealth, prosperity (both material and spiritual), fortune and the embodiment of beauty. She is the consort of the god Vishnu. A popular name for Hindu temples and children.

Lath Mar Holi a local celebration of the Hindu festival of Holi (q.v.) that takes place in advance of Holi in the town of Barsana in the state of Uttar Pradesh. Translating as 'Holi in which people hit with sticks', the tradition is based on the legend that Lord Krishna visited his beloved Radha's village (according to legend at Barsana) and playfully teased her and her friends. Taking offence at this, the women of Barsana chased him away. Since then, men from Krishna's village, Nandgaon, visit Barsana to play Holi (re-enacting the incident with laths, or wooden truncheons) in the town that has the distinction of having the only temple dedicated to Radha in India.

lingam a cosmic pillar of fire, a representation of the god Shiva, often worshipped in temples and family homes, which scholars interpret as symbolic of the male sexual organs (*see also* yoni).

Maharaja a Sanskrit title for 'great king' or 'high king', in prevalent use from the medieval era onwards to refer to the rulers of India's princely states. On the eve of Indian independence in 1927, India (including modern-day Pakistan and Bangladesh) contained 600 princely states.

maithuna a Sanskrit term often translated as sexual union in a ritual context. Also used in reference to the amorously entwined couples in sculptural friezes in Hindu temples such as those at Khajuraho.

moksha, mukti the liberation from samsara, the cycle of death or rebirth.

Mughal India a Persianate empire that ruled large parts of the Indian subcontinent from 1526 to 1737 and was at its peak under the 49-year reign of the expansionist (and pious Muslim) Aurangzeb (1618–1707).

neem Indian lilac, a tree in the mahogany family, native to the Indian subcontinent. For two millennia, the products of the 'Sacred Tree' have been used for medicinal and cosmetic purposes, including as a sedative, contraceptive and for topical skin treatment. A common ingredient in modern mass-produced cosmetics.

NRI non-resident Indian, a citizen of India who holds an Indian passport and has temporarily emigrated to another country for six months or longer. A status used legally for the purpose of income tax gathering. Distinct from a person of Indian origin (PIO), whose ancestors were born in India but who is a citizen of another country.

paan from the Sanskrit parna, meaning feather or leaf, a stimulating, psychoactive preparation of betel leaf combined with areca nut and/or tobacco and various additions, including fennel seed to freshen the breath. Paan is chewed and finally spat out or swallowed.

paneer an acid-set (without rennet, therefore fully lacto vegetarian) fresh cheese common in south Asian cuisine.

Purity Movement, Social Purity Movement a late nineteenth-century social movement that sought to abolish prostitution and other sexual activities that were considered immoral according to the interpretation of Christian doctrine. Composed primarily of women, the movement was active in English-speaking nations from the late 1860s to about 1910, exerting an influence on the feminist, eugenics and birth control movements.

Qutbh Shah Muhammad Quli Qutb Shah (1580–1612 CE), the fifth sultan of the Turkic Qutb Shahi dynasty of Golkonda and founder of the city of Hyderabad, an able administrator whose reign is considered one of the high points of the Qutb Shahi dynasty. A scholar of Arabic and Persian, he wrote celebrated poetry in Urdu.

Rama the seventh avatar of the god Vishnu and a popular figure and deity in Hinduism, Rama is the central figure of Hindu epic the Ramayana (one of the two great epics of India, along with the Mahabharata). In the Ramayana, in which Rama fights a terrible war in exile from his wife Sita in order to rescue his wife and their honour, he is depicted as a perfect adherent to dharma (q.v.) despite the harsh tests of life and time.

sadhu a wandering Hindu ascetic, or monk, whose life is dedicated to pursuing moksha (q.v.).

Saraswati the Hindu goddess of knowledge, music, arts and science and companion to Brahma. Revered by believers in Jainism (q.v.).

Sati Hindu goddess of marital fidelity and first consort to Shiva. Otherwise known as Dakshayani. The illegal act of sati, in which a Hindu widow immolates herself on her husband's funeral pyre as a final and consummate act of loyalty and devotion, is patterned after the deed committed by this goddess to uphold the honour of her husband.

Sepoy Mutiny British Raj name for what is now called the Indian Rebellion of 1857 (or India's First War of Independence), which began as a mutiny of sepoys (Indian soldiers in the pay of a European power) in the East India Company's army and escalated to hostilities in present-day Uttar Pradesh, Bihar, northern Madhya Pradesh and the Delhi region. The mutiny was the result of various grievances, including the sepoys being asked to bite off the paper cartridges for their rifles, which they believed were greased with animal fat. The rebellion was contained with the fall of Gwalior on 20 June 1858 and led to the dissolution of the East India Company (q.v.) in 1858. It also led the direct governance of India by the British Crown as the new British Raj.

Shakti the primordial cosmic energy, or divine feminine creative force, that is believed in Hinduism to move through the entire universe and be responsible for creation and change.

shalwar kameez a modest and traditional dress worn by both women and men in South Asia and parts of Central Asia, featuring loose pyjama-like trousers (shalwar), which narrow at the ankle, and a long skirt or tunic, often with side seams (kameez).

Shankar, Ravi an Indian musician and composer (1920–2012) who played the sitar and achieved global fame in the 1960s. The Beatles' George Harrison studied sitar under Shankar for six weeks in June 1966.

Shiva a Hindu deity considered the supreme god in Shaivism, one of the three most influential denominations of Hinduism. Often represented by the form of the lingam (q.v.).

Sita in Hinduism an avatar of Lakshmi and the embodiment of perfect womanhood. Consort to Rama and central to the Indian epic Ramayana.

sutra in Sanskrit literally a thread or line; in its literary usage an aphorism or collection of such aphorisms in a Hindu or Buddhist text.

Tantra a style of meditation and ritual practice that arose in India around the fifth century CE. Its rituals and philosophy influenced, and were absorbed by, Hindu, Sikh, Buddhist and Jain traditions and spread from South to Southeast Asia. Tantra was at its zenith during the Gupta Empire (q.v.).

tilak in Hinduism a mark worn on the forehead and other parts of the body on a daily basis or for special religious occasions only, depending on discrete custom.

twank an over-the-hill twink (q.v.).

twink Western urban gay slang for an attractive boyish-looking, spritish young man, usually of slender build.

Veda a large body of texts originating in ancient India (1500–500 BCE) and constituting the oldest layer of Sanskrit literature and the oldest scriptures of Hinduism; also refers to the Vedic period, which roughly spans from the Late Bronze Age to the Iron Age.

viceroy a regal official who runs a country, colony or city province in the name of and as representative of the ruling overseas monarch.

Vishnu the Vedic supreme god in Hinduism and the supreme being in Vaishnavism. His ten avatars include Varaha, the boar, and Matsya, the fish.

wallah derived from Hindustani, a suffix indicating a person involved in some type of service or activity, such as dabbawallah (lunchbox deliverer) or chaiwallah (tea seller).

wheatish having a light brown or creamy light brown complexion.

yoni Sanskrit word for the vagina, also a symbol of Shakti, or the divine feminine creative force. The counterpart to the lingam (q.v.) and often combined with the lingam in artistic and sculptural representations.

Bibliography

Anon. (2009) *The Mahabharata*, trans. John D. Smith, Penguin Classics.

Bhasin, Raaja (1994) *Shimla: The Summer Capital of British India*, Penguin.

Boo, Katherine (2012) *Behind the Beautiful Forevers: Life, Death and Hope in a Mumbai Slum*, Random House.

Chakravarthy, Pritham K. & Khanna, Rakesh (2011) *The Blaft Anthology of Tamil Pulp Fiction*, Blaft Publications.

Chaudhry, Minakshi (2010) *Love Stories of Shimla Hills*, Rupa.

Chaudhuri, Amit (2011) An Infatuation, *London Review of Books*.

Chopra, Ashok (ed.) (2011) *Khushwant Singh on Women Sex, Love and Lust*, Hay House.

Dallapiccola, A.L. (2013) *Indian Love Poetry*, British Museum Press.

de Courcy, Anne (2012) *The Fishing Fleet: Husband-Hunting in the Raj*, Weidenfeld & Nicolson.

Doyle, Laura (2001) *The Surrendered Wife: A Step by Step Guide to Finding Intimacy, Passion and Peace with Your Man*, Simon & Schuster.

Halve, Anand and Sarkar, Anita (2012) *Adkatha: The Story of Indian Advertising*, New Delhi Sage Response.

Harford, Tim (2008) *The Logic of Life: Uncovering the New Economics of Everything*, Little, Brown.

Hyam, Ronald (1991) *Empire and Sexuality*, St Martin's Press.

Hyam, Ronald (2010) *Understanding the British Empire*, Cambridge University Press.

Jha, Anjani Kumar (2011) *Aghoreshwar*, Rema Ram Temple Publishing.

Kakar, Sudhir (1990) *Intimate Relations: Exploring Indian Sexuality*, University of Chicago Press.

Kesavan, Mukul (2008) *The Ugliness of the Indian Male and Other Propositions*, Black Kite.

Kipling, Rudyard (1999) *The Collected Poems of Rudyard Kipling*, Wordsworth Editions.

Lewis, C.S. (1936) *The Allegory of Love: A Study in Medieval Tradition*, Oxford University Press.

Menen, Rajendar (2012) *Karma Sutra: Adventures of a Street Bum*, HarperCollins India.

Mishra, Pankah (2006) *Butter Chicken in Ludhiana: Travels in Small Town India*, Picador.

Odzer, Cleo (1995) *Goa Freaks: My Hippie Years in India*, Foxrock.

Picard, Liza (2005) *Victorian London, The Life of a City 1840–1870*, Orion.

Porter, Roy & Teich, Mikulas (1994) *Sexual Knowledge, Sexual Science: The History of Attitudes to Sexuality*, Cambridge University Press.

Radhakrishna, Geeta & Menon, R.K. (1997) *Mohiniyattam: The Dance of the Enchantress*, Mohiniatta Nritya Kalakshetra.

Robb, Peter (ed.) (2011) *Sex and Sensibility: Richard Blechynden's Calcutta Diaries 1791–1822*, OUP India.

Rose, Phyllis (1984) *Parallel Lives: Five Victorian Marriages*, Vintage.

Rosin, Hanna (2012) *The End of Men: And the Rise of Women*, Riverhead Books.

Roy, Rahul (2007) *A Little Book on Men*, Yoda Press.

Russell, Bertrand (1929) *Marriage and Morals*, George Allen and Unwin.

Vatsyayana, Mallanaga (1995) *The Kama Sutra*, trans. Sir Richard Burton, Wordsworth Classics.

Vatsyayana, Mallanaga (2002) *Kamasutra*, trans. Wendy Doniger & Sudhir Kakar, Oxford World's Classics.

Vatsyayana, Mallanaga (2011) *The Kama Sutra: A Guide to the Art of Pleasure*, trans. A.N.D. Haksar, Penguin.

Von Tunzelmann, Alex (2007) *Indian Summer: The Secret History of the End of an Empire*, Picador.

Zaidi, Annie & Revindra, Smriti (2011) *The Bad Boy's Guide to the Good Indian Girl*, Zubaan.

Acknowledgements

Thanks to Nicholas Brealey for taking a risk on a project whose topicality – while now self-evident – was less so when the idea for *The Kama Sutra Diaries* first took shape.

Thanks, in India, to Geetanjali Krishna for her generosity with story leads, to Raaja Bhasin for his depth of knowledge on the Indian Raj, to Rosalyn d'Mello for the heads-up on Indian feminism, to Meenakshi Puri, Kapil Gaba, Pragya Taneja and Mala Sachdeva for the insight into the intersection between modern Indian spirituality and sexuality. To Kirat Sodhi for the impromptu photography services at Khajuraho. To Rajendar Menen for being so generous with his opinions and research on Mumbai's red-light district. To Lisa Marbaniang and Mary for their welcome at Shillong. And to Priya Paul for background knowledge on the Indian marriage market.

Thanks, in the UK, to Anne and John for the supper-making services and giving me the space to write. Thanks to Tim Davies, Stacey Teale, Tanya Love, Gemma Elwin-Harris, Prudence Korda, Anna Watson, Adam Howard, Kate Mansfield, Sophy Grimshaw, Sarah Costley and all at Studio 20 for their support, proofing, read-throughs and feedback through the endless drafting stages. To Susannah Lear, Sally Lansdell and all at Nicholas Brealey for their hard work with the drafts and design. To Nick Black for his insights into the 1960s sexual revolution. Thanks to Nomi Kakoty at Dalton Kakoty and all at Greaves Travel, Cox and Kings, Abercrombie & Kent and Taj and Oberoi Hotels for allowing me to cannibalise my travel journalism contacts in pursuit of this project.

Every effort has been made to assure the accuracy of all facts in these pages, but mistakes have doubtless crept in (for which I accept full responsibility). Some of the names and key details about the subjects and interviewees featured in *The Kama Sutra Diaries* have been changed in an effort to protect privacy or at the subject's request.